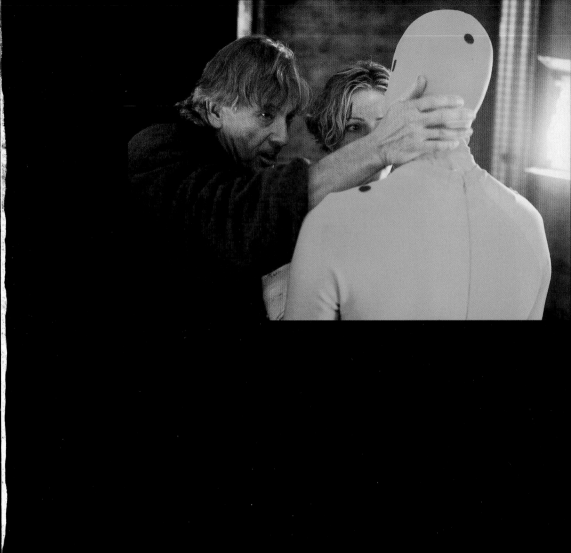

PAUL VERHOEVEN

FRONT COVER
Still from 'RoboCop' (1987)
RoboCop is an American Jesus with a gun, who is crucified and then resurrected, and kills rather than arrests.

FIRST PAGE
On the set of 'Hollow Man' (2000)
An intense Paul Verhoeven directs Kevin Bacon (in green suit) and Elizabeth Shue.

FRONTISPIECE
On the set of 'Spetters' (1980)
Verhoeven spends some time collecting his thoughts before embarking on the next shot. Assistant Hans Kemma, who had worked with Verhoeven since 'Floris', remembers that he would call "Silence on the set! The director is thinking!" and a few moments later Verhoeven would come up with a solution to whatever visual problem had presented itself.

THIS PAGE
1 On the set of 'RoboCop' (1987) Verhoeven in front of the ED-209, the mindless law-enforcement robot. Verhoeven turned a comic-book movie into a social satire of America during the Reagan era.

2 On the set of 'Total Recall' (1990) Arnold Schwarzenegger and Sharon Stone look at a monitor to see how Verhoeven wants the fight between them choreographed.

OPPOSITE
On the set of 'Starship Troopers' (1997)
Filming the soldiers attacking the bugs in this ironic adaptation of Robert Heinlein's classic SF novel.

PAGES 6/7
On the set of 'Hollow Man' (2000)
Paul Verhoeven shows the gorilla how to roar.

BACK COVER
Paul Verhoeven

To stay informed about upcoming TASCHEN titles, please request our magazine at www.taschen.com or write to TASCHEN America, 6671 Sunset Boulevard, Suite 1508, Los Angeles, CA 90028, USA, Fax: +1-323-463.4442. We will be happy to send you a free copy of our magazine which is filled with information about all of our books.

© 2005 TASCHEN GmbH
Hohenzollernring 53, D–50672 Köln
www.taschen.com
Editor/Picture Research/Layout/Captions: Paul Duncan/Wordsmith Solutions
Editorial Coordination: Michael Cramm, Cologne
Production Coordination: Tina Ciborowius, Cologne
Typeface Design: Sense/Net, Andy Disl, Cologne

Printed in Italy
ISBN 3–8228–3101–8

Notes
A superscript number indicates a reference to a note on page 191

Image sources
Paul Verhoeven, Los Angeles: 1, 2, 4right, 5, 6/7, 10top, 11, 13(2), 14, 16bottom, 17, 26, 27(2), 28, 40, 41(2), 42, 45, 49t, 51, 52, 54r, 56t, 58t, 59b, 61, 62, 63(2), 64, 65, 74, 75, 76(2), 77r, 79, 80top left + top right, 81, 85, 93(2), 96b, 98bl+br, 102, 108b, 109tl+b, 110r, 111, 112(3), 113(2), 114(2), 116t, 117(2), 118, 122b, 123(2), 128r, 133(2), 134, 140, 142/143, 143, 148l+tr, 150, 151(2), 152t, 154(4), 155t, 156(2), 159t, 162bl+br, 163b, 164(2), 165, 167(2), 172, 174(2), 175(2), 176, 177(2), 180l, 182(2), 183(2), 184(2), 185(2), 188l, 192
PWE Verlag / defd-movies, Hamburg: Front Cover, 4l, 10b, 15t, 16tr, 18t, 19, 38t, 47, 49bl, 50b, 53, 56b, 68, 69(2), 72b, 73b, 86, 90(2), 91b, 92, 94, 98t, 100, 103t, 104t, 105t, 106, 107, 108tr, 109tr, 110l, 115t, 120 (2), 124, 125, 126, 127, 131, 132, 135, 137t, 138, 141, 146, 148/149b, 158(2), 162t, 163t, 166, 168, 169, 170, 171, 173(2), 178, 179, 180/181, 189l
Amsterdam Filmmuseum: 16tl, 18b, 20, 22, 23, 24, 25, 34, 35, 36, 37(2), 38b, 39, 44, 49br, 54l, 55(2), 57, 60, 66, 67(2), 70, 71b, 73t, 80bl, 82, 83, 88, 89, 186(3), 187(2), 188r
British Film Institute Stills, Posters and Designs, London: 8, 46, 58b, 59t, 87, 96t, 97b, 100bl, 103b, 105b, 108tl, 116b, 119, 137b, 146/147, 155b, 159b
Photofest, New York: 15b, 71t, 72t, 91t, 100t+br, 101, 104b, 115b, 121, 122t, 128tl+bl, 129, 130, 152b, 160 (2), 161
The Kobal Collection, London/New York: 77l, 78, 80bl, 84, 97t
Instituut voor beeld en geluid, Hilversum: 30, 31, 32(2), 33
Herbert Klemens/Filmbild Fundus Robert Fischer, München: 50t

CONTENTS

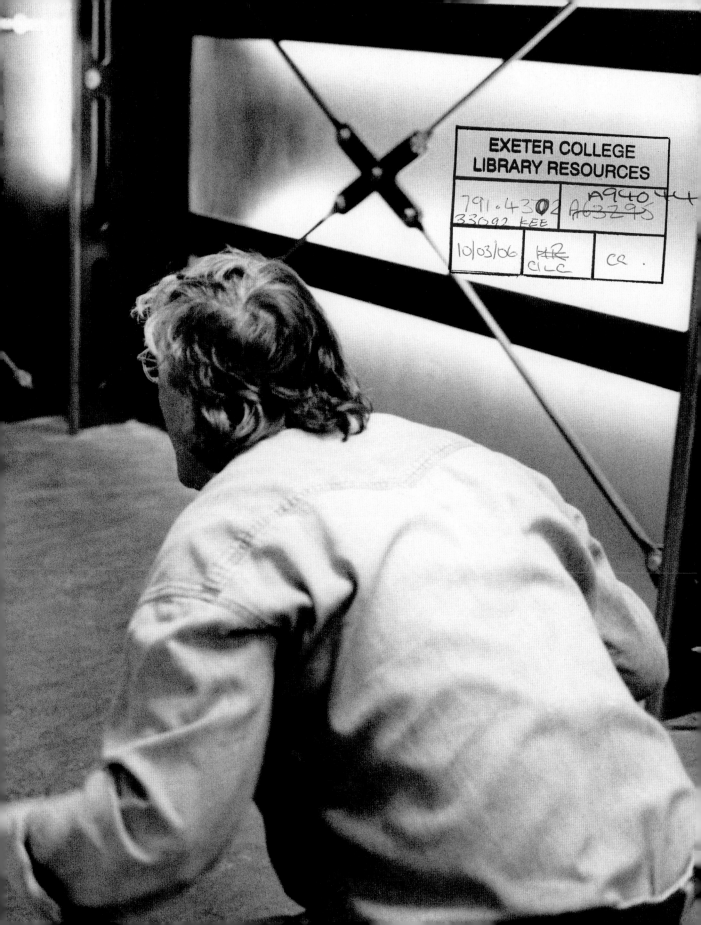

Introduction
"We Must Acknowledge These Dark Things"

From his early films made in the Netherlands, including *Turkish Delight* and *Spetters*, to such Hollywood movies as *Total Recall*, *Basic Instinct*, *Showgirls* and *Starship Troopers*, Paul Verhoeven has been a centre of controversy for the graphic sex and violence in his films. As interviewer Dennis Lim has noted, 'No other film-maker with massive budgets to blow is as reflexively sardonic, amusingly smut-minded, or pathologically tasteless, and the epithets have been far-ranging: mad scientist, evil genius, porn peddler, misogynist, homophobe, dirty old man, Nazi.'[1] Over the years, Verhoeven has received quite a drubbing from hostile critics who have accused him of sadism and sexploitation. Terrence Rafferty wrote about *Total Recall* that it is 'full of relentless action and spectacular effects, and it's no fun at all. ... [The] picture itself is a terminator: when it's over, you feel as if the life has been pounded out of you, and you never want to go to the movies again.'[2] David Thomson described *RoboCop*, *Total Recall* and *Basic Instinct* as 'three authentic smash hits, all three violent, nasty, and flirting with the inhuman,'[3] while Richard Schickel attacked *Hollow Man* for having 'too much pornographically arranged death.'[4] In her review of *Showgirls*, Claire Monk wrote that 'after two hours the film's relentless tits-in-your-face display – intensified by Verhoeven's trademark high-impact visuals – comes to feel like a never-ending nightmare.'[5] And according to Richard Corliss, 'For 2 hrs. 11 min., *Showgirls* offers a slumming party inside the moviemakers' libidos. Ladies and gents, no matter how curious or horny you think you are, you don't want to be there.'[6]

Verhoeven has been a staunch defender of his films against the charge that they promote violence between men or against women. The director has noted that psychological studies show "a definite correlation between violence in films and violent people, in that violent films tend to attract violent people. But there is gigantic confusion in this country [the US] about the difference between correlation and causation! There is no evidence that violence in films *causes* people to become violent. The same violent American movies go to Western Europe, and viewers there don't seem to have any violent reactions! They're watching the same movies! The only difference between the United States and Western Europe is that in Western Europe, you cannot get a gun."[7] Verhoeven has made this same point more pithily in arguing that "One automatic weapon has more influence than 100 movies."[8] In fact, Verhoeven maintains that politicians and other powerbrokers in America blame

Still from 'RoboCop' (1987)
Many images and events in Verhoeven's films resonate with images and events of Christian mythology. Murphy is killed by thugs and then resurrected as RoboCop. Here RoboCop goes through the fires of 'HELL'.

"When the other kids were playing with a ball, all I wanted to do was take the ball and throw it in the water. That was my game. I thought it was fun to disrupt the game, to change it."

Paul Verhoeven

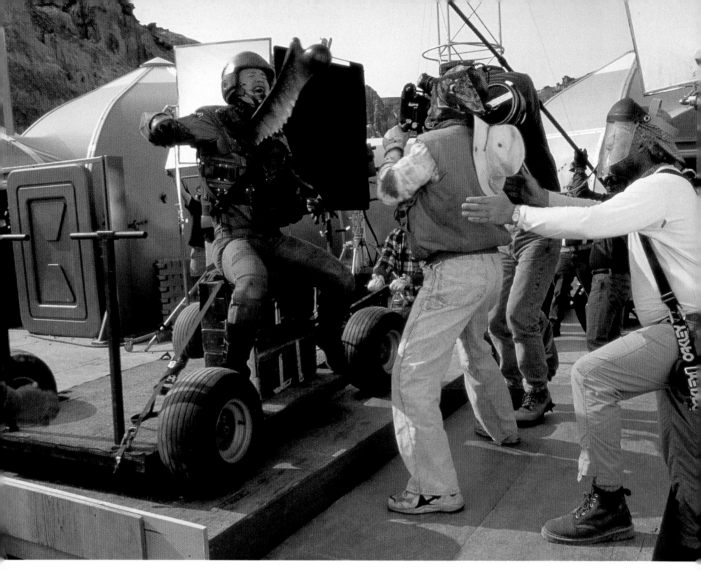

ABOVE
On the set of 'Starship Troopers' (1997)
Paul Verhoeven is a visceral film-maker who shows sex and violence as it really happens. In 'Starship Troopers' many of the cast get sliced to pieces by the bugs. Here Dizzy Flores (Dina Meyer) gets spiked by a bug.

RIGHT
On the set of 'Starship Troopers' (1997)
Kevin Yagher, who created many of the puppets for the film, shows the remains of a trooper whose head is sliced off by a flying bug.

OPPOSITE
On the set of 'Starship Troopers' (1997)
Shaun Smith and Kevin Yagher prepare the Lt. Jean Rasczak puppet. Rasczak has been sucked down a bug hole and had his legs bitten off. The camera crew are wearing goggles to protect themselves from the blood spraying out of the leg stumps.

Hollywood for the violence in society so that they will not have to do anything about the real causes: "the film industry will then serve as a scapegoat for society's distress. The debate distracts attention from America's real problems – where the violence is caused by economic decline, drugs and that idiotic firearms law. As long as you can buy a revolver here for next to nothing, people will continue to shoot each other – but they would rather not talk about that."[9]

But Verhoeven *will* talk about it – about the easy availability of weapons and the damage they do to the body. In *Starship Troopers*, a satiric newsbreak shows soldiers letting kids handle their guns and watching them fight over who gets to hold the weapons. Some critics said that younger viewers would misunderstand the film as promoting violence, but Verhoeven watched the film with kids in the audience and has said that "They all got the message; they all start laughing. They realize we're saying, 'Everybody has a gun in this country.' I think they all see the irony."[10] This irony becomes even more apparent when the film's high school-age heroes go patriotically off to war and are then horribly mutilated in combat, some literally ripped to shreds. These dismembered bodies are the reality of war, and Verhoeven's credo is to show this reality for what it is: "I like always to push the edges in every direction, in a moral way, in a sexual way, in a way of action and violence. I always feel that it's never enough. I always feel 'can we do more, can we be closer to reality?' Because if you see someone who is wounded or loses an arm in battle, for instance, and what it does to somebody, well, that's never been portrayed on the screen; it has not, not even nearly."[11]

While most Hollywood science-fiction films such as *Star Wars* or *Independence Day* present violence as relatively clean, distant and enjoyable, Verhoeven emphasizes the bloody, assaultive and excruciating truth about violence, as in the horrific scenes of Murphy's dismemberment in *RoboCop*, Richter's amputated arms in *Total Recall* and the soldiers torn apart in *Starship Troopers*. "There is a lot of opening of the human body in my movies," Verhoeven has said; "I'm very sensitive to the weakness and the vulnerability of the human body."[12] By getting graphically physical about the impact of violence on flesh and blood, Verhoeven adds a savage realism to science fiction, a genre that is usually escapist in its avoidance of the facts about trauma and suffering. Verhoeven has said that he likes to take a "B-genre" like science fiction and "elevate" it using "hyperbole and irony and [Brechtian] alienation" so that it becomes "a vehicle for other thoughts,"[13] such as a critique of pro-gun policies and gung-ho militarism. The visceral violence in Verhoeven's films explodes the B-movie myths of a typical action-adventure, revealing that the "just a scratch" wounds and sanitized suffering of most Hollywood films are a lie. Verhoeven has described himself as a director who is "provocative" in the sense that he "explores the difference between reality and the way in which we usually see reality portrayed. I feel that there is a huge discrepancy between what life really is and what we are supposed to see in the movies."[14]

It is not just in cases of violence, but also in matters of sex that Verhoeven shows us what we are not "supposed" to see – aspects of our physical lives that are normally censored from Hollywood films. Verhoeven's description of his Dutch film *Spetters* can be taken as a general statement about his approach to sexuality in all of his films: "I wanted to go beyond what was normal, what you would normally see on the screen. I wanted to show things that are true and real but that are normally omitted. I wanted to say if it's true, then I'll shoot it, and I'll shoot it the way it's done. I'm not going to be elliptic or shoot it in a way you don't see it, in the dark or

ABOVE
Still from 'Soldier of Orange' (1977)
Guus LeJeune (Jeroen Krabbé) and Erik Lanshof (Rutger Hauer) are Dutch students who thought it would be an adventure to fight the Germans during World War Two. However, Guus and most of Erik's other friends die during the war.

LEFT
Still from 'Soldier of Orange' (1977)
For Erik, part of the adventure is to seduce women like Esther (Belinda Meuldijk), his friend's fiancée.

On the set of 'Starship Troopers' (1997)
Paul Verhoeven on the Whiskey Outpost set. As
a child during World War Two he had seen dead
and dismembered bodies and all his films
remain true to those initial visions of violence.

*"I am a passionate advocate of freedom of
expression. The moment you talk of
responsibilities it raises the question of who is to
say what is negative and what happens to those
who make negative things. What committee is to
decide? If Michael Medved had his way,
Shakespeare would never have been allowed to
have produced* Hamlet— *there are too many
deaths."*

Paul Verhoeven

TOP
On the set of 'Starship Troopers' (1997)
The bugs did not exist, so every shot had to be carefully planned. Here Verhoeven explains the positions of the characters and bugs to cinematographer Jost Vacano and producer Alan Marshall.

ABOVE
On the set of 'Starship Troopers' (1997)
Verhoeven shows Patrick Muldoon how and where he wants him to shoot. In this scene he is giving covering fire whilst the troopers pile into the aircraft behind him.

Women

Verhoeven's films are full of strong women. As Renée Soutendijk put it: "Most of the women in Paul's films will not rest until they have got what they want. They usually win, and they let no one stand in their way."

Above: 'Katie Tippel' (1975) Katie Tippel (Monique van de Ven) has nothing to offer but her beauty as she climbs the social ladder from bread-stealing hunger to a life of luxury as the wife of a rich socialist.

Top Right: 'Basic Instinct' (1992) Femme fatale Catherine Tramell (Sharon Stone) has lots of money, a successful writing career, many willing sexual partners of differing orientations, and gets away with murder. She is completely free.

Right: 'Spetters' (1980) Fientje (Renée Soutendijk) sleeps with promising young men so that she can get money and security, but moves to another man if the previous one fails. She starts by selling french fries in a trailer and ends by selling french fries in a disco bar.

Opposite: 'Showgirls' (1995) Nomi (Elizabeth Berkley) hitch-hikes into town with the intention of becoming the biggest dancer in Las Vegas.

ABOVE
Still from 'Spetters' (1980)
Verhoeven is no stranger to controversy because
his films contain sexual acts that some members
of society would prefer not to be presented to
the general public. In 'Spetters', for example, Eef
(Toon Agterberg, left) beats up and robs gays, is
gang-raped by gays, and then comes out as gay.
In this scene, Eef watches two gays having oral
sex. Verhoeven hired an easy-going gay couple
for the performance. When he yelled "Cut!" the
men turned around angrily because the 'client'
had not come yet.

RIGHT
Protests against 'Spetters' (1980)
The Nederlandse Anti-Spetters Actie (NASA)
was formed in protest at Verhoeven's depiction
of women (Fientje sleeps around), homosexuals
(Eef acknowledges his homosexuality after he is
gang-raped) and people in wheelchairs (Rien
commits suicide when he loses the use of his
legs). Essentially, they were complaining that the
film reflected the lack of hope in the working-
class youths at that time.

in the shadows, I'll shoot it straight. This is how people give a blow job, and this is how they rape, and this is how they masturbate, this is how you jerk off somebody, and you see it all. That's just the reality of life."[15] Unlike the romanticized prostitution in such films as *Pretty Woman* (1990) or the faux scandal of a movie like *Dirty Dancing* (1987), Verhoeven's *Showgirls* is disturbingly explicit about what Nomi does with her body to satisfy men's lust as she strips, lap-dances and screws her way to the top. Where most Hollywood romances, melodramas, and even thrillers idealize sex as softcore lovemaking or cut away from sexual violence before it becomes too graphic, Verhoeven toughens these genres with a new realism, as in the nakedly joyous coupling of Erik and Olga in *Turkish Delight* or, on the dark side, the viciously visualized rapes of Katie in *Katie Tippel*, Agnes in *Flesh+Blood* and Molly in *Showgirls*. Sexual assault is part of reality, and Verhoeven refuses to soften or censor it into something more "acceptable" or less "offensive" than it actually is: "Rape is an animalistic, aggressive, intruding evil behaviour. And I portray rape in my movies [in these terrible ways] because I disagree [with it]."[16] As with war's violence, rape's violation of the body must be graphically presented or the film is a lie.

Verhoeven is also one of very few directors to show full-frontal male nudity, including the flaccid organs of Erik in *Turkish Delight*, Gerard in *The Fourth Man* and Johnny Boz in *Basic Instinct* – all men who are vulnerable to castration anxiety and a fear of the female sex. This fear can lead to violence against women. For example, the rape of Katie in *Katie Tippel* and the invisible man's rape of a neighbour in *Hollow Man*. Where other directors follow the Hollywood convention of showing women nude but covering up for the men, Verhoeven insists on exposing the male organ as a sign of men's vulnerability and violent rage. As he says about the rapist in *Hollow Man*, "Sebastian becomes evil because there is a shadow inside him like in all of us,"[17] and "We must acknowledge these dark things because the sooner we admit our capacity for evil the less apt we are to destroy each other."[18]

This last statement by Verhoeven can stand as a rationale for his realistic approach to sex and violence, for it is only by breaking through our idealistic lies about ourselves that we can understand who we truly are and how much better we could become. Verhoeven's sensationalism is precise and significant: the flesh and blood of his images – their frankness and gore – are attempts to restore *realism* to conventional genres that have been spreading *myths* about sex and violence. While Hollywood films often seem to present cartoon violence that has no effect on the invincible body of the male hero, Verhoeven forces us to "see what happens to someone's organs, flesh and bones when something violent happens."[19] Similarly, while many mainstream movies show partial nudity or softcore sex for titillation, Verhoeven's harder, more explicit approach exposes those other films for what they are: romanticized, prettified lies or myths about a subject – sex – that has a deeper and often darker meaning, as in sexual paranoia or predation. According to film journalist Paul M. Sammon, 'The public persona that Paul Verhoeven has is of this kind of like barely contained wild man who's always out there trying to show full-frontal fornication and decapitations every moment he can. That may, in an exaggerated way, be a part of Paul's personality, but Paul is also a very serious and a very intelligent man.'[20] It is Verhoeven's serious, intelligent treatment of sex and violence that is the main subject of this book.

Still from 'Katie Tippel' (1975)
In his Dutch films, Verhoeven presents nudity naturally and does not idealise it. People come in all shapes and sizes.

A Young Man
1938–1973

Paul Verhoeven was born in Amsterdam on 18 July 1938. The Germans invaded the Netherlands in 1940. Between the ages of two and seven, the young Verhoeven witnessed summary executions of Dutch people by their Nazi occupiers, and Allied planes bombing and being shot down close to where he and his parents lived: "In my town, people were literally starving, dead bodies were scattered around the streets, windows would blow out all over us at dinner as the bombing started and planes crashed in flames on top of houses... When you are a kid, living in such a world is such a shock that it never really wears off... I think it's the origin of my adult fascination with violence."[21] Unlike in most movies where violence is either softened to lessen its impact or else exaggerated for comic-book effect, the violence in Verhoeven's films is graphic and visceral because he refuses to lie about the devastation it does to the body. As he has explained, "I prefer to show things instead of depicting them elliptically or suggesting them... My tendency is to be ultra-realistic with... violence."[22] *Starship Troopers* may be only a science-fiction adventure, but Verhoeven has directed the battle scenes so that they are "disorienting, terrifying and bloody, just like real combat itself."[23] Editor Mark Goldblatt says that Verhoeven "pulls no punches. So when a violent moment occurs, say during a Bug attack, Paul will allow the viewer to experience it in a very visceral way. ... *Starship Troopers* is a war film, right? And war, as they say, is Hell."[24]

During the Nazi occupation, the young Verhoeven saw a number of pro-fascist propaganda films, which he would later satirize in *Starship Troopers*. After the war, Dutch cinemas were flooded with American genre films – Westerns, action-adventures, and sci-fi such as *The Crimson Pirate* (1952) and *The War of the Worlds* (1953). It was at this point, as a boy and then a teenager that Verhoeven first thought of becoming a movie director. He was good at drawing, having tried his hand at several amateur comic strips – a skill which he would later use extensively when drawing detailed storyboards for his films. In 1955, aged 17, Verhoeven attended art school in Paris. The unflinching realism of Dutch paintings by Rembrandt and Hieronymus Bosch had a profound effect on him. Such pictures as one of a vagabond pissing against a brothel wall, or another of two people making love while behind them two dogs are mating, displayed a frankness about physical matters which Verhoeven would adopt for his own films. Verhoeven wanted to go

On the set of 'One Lizard Too Many' (1960)
22-year-old mathematics student Paul Verhoeven made films in his spare time.

"In our deepest being we are no more than a piece of flesh."
Paul Verhoeven

On the set of 'One Lizard Too Many' (1960)
After making a short film about two teacups, a ghostly figure and a spoon that seemed to have moved, Verhoeven won the competition to make a film for the Leiden Student Association's anniversary celebration. It was filmed in student rooms and on the streets of Leiden in the spirit of the emerging French New Wave. Verhoeven is on the left.

Still from 'One Lizard Too Many' (1960)

A film about identity. A wife (Hermine Menalda) has a relationship with a student (Erik Bree) because her sculptor husband cannot make a bust of her face. The husband makes a bust of how he sees his wife rather than how she really is. The student's girlfriend (Marijke Jones), who looks like the wife, dresses as the wife and poses for the husband.

Still from 'The Hitchhikers' (1962)
In this short film, three boys pick up a girl and
compete for her affection.

to film school in Paris, but unfortunately he missed the application deadline. Besides, his father told him he would be foolish to pursue a film-making career when there was virtually no film industry in the Netherlands at that time.

His father, who was headmaster at a primary school, convinced Verhoeven that he should attend the University of Leiden in the Netherlands (1956-1964) and prepare to enter a more respectable profession with a steadier income, such as becoming a mathematics professor. Verhoeven would eventually earn a Ph.D. in mathematics and physics, with a special interest in Einstein's theory of relativity. This training would not only help him to understand the complexities of the special effects in his later science-fiction films, it also enabled him to comprehend the intricacies of different character perspectives and interconnected storylines in his often ambiguous movies: "Scientifically, there is no such thing as one reality. There are many versions of reality which exist at the same time. This is a principle I consider fundamental in my life and therefore in my films. In *Showgirls* for example, Zack, Cristal and Nomi are all three convinced they control the game, and each of them is right from their point of view."[25]

At the university, Verhoeven joined the elite Leiden Studenten Corps (Leiden Student Association) and was subjected to humiliating hazing rituals like those he would later depict in *Soldier of Orange*. It was also at Leiden that the future director of *Basic Instinct* attended a student party where a young woman unabashedly

On the set of 'The Hitchhikers' (1962)
For his early films, Verhoeven learned a lot from working with experienced cameraman Frits Boersma. Here Verhoeven is hidden behind the girl in the car, and is holding a mirror so that he can see what is being shot.

revealed that she was wearing no underwear when she deliberately uncrossed her legs in front of a blushing Verhoeven and his friend.

Verhoeven saw films by directors who would have a lasting influence on his work. The gritty realism of Ingmar Bergman's depiction of the Middle Ages in *The Seventh Seal* (*Det sjunde inseglet*, 1957) would be an inspiration for *Flesh+Blood*. Billy Wilder's satiric bite would be a reference for *RoboCop* and *Starship Troopers*. The battle scenes in these two science-fiction films owed a great deal to the way action was shot by Akira Kurosawa (*Seven Samurai, Shichinin no samurai*, 1954) and David Lean (*The Bridge on the River Kwai*, 1957 and *Doctor Zhivago*, 1965). Verhoeven's penchant for fluid camerawork and choreographed character movements found inspiration in Federico Fellini's *8 1/2* (1963) and Orson Welles' *Touch of Evil* (1958). And then there is Alfred Hitchcock, the most direct and profound influence on Verhoeven in terms of suspenseful cutting style, menacing camera movement, and (sometimes) high or low angles on the action: "I studied *Vertigo* [1958]. I must have seen it at least fifteen times. I know every shot of the movie by heart and entire scenes from *Vertigo* came back [in my mind] while I was shooting *Basic Instinct*"[26]; "I think every movie of Hitchcock you can study forever and you will always find things that you can use yourself."[27]

Verhoeven joined the Leiden film club. Having been given a 16mm movie camera by his uncle at age 17, he already had some experience making home movies with his parents and friends. Now, with the help of his fellow students at Leiden, Verhoeven would begin to develop his craft in earnest by directing four short films. *One Lizard Too Many* (*Een Hagedis Teveel*, 1960) has elements of *Vertigo*. Just as Scottie (James Stewart) desires the mysterious and elusive Madeleine more than the ordinary, available Judy (Kim Novak in both roles), so an artist sculpts the desirable faces of other women, but not that of his wife. The fact that two lizards crawl through the film shows the influence of Surrealist painting, which interested Verhoeven at the time. After this short film won first prize at an international student film festival Verhoeven decided to choose film-making over painting as a career.

Still from 'Let's Have a Party' (1963)
This short film shows the friendship between boys at school and their affection for girls.

Nothing Special (*Niets Bijzonders*, 1961) shows a young man in a café, enjoying a meditative smoke while imagining that an identical twin is dating his girlfriend in his place. The film is based on an idea of William Faulkner's that if a man could watch himself being intimate with a woman, he would laugh so much he would never have sex again. *The Hitchhikers* (*De Lifters*, 1962) is about three boys in a Studebaker competing for the affections of a girl. *Let's Have a Party* (*Feest*, 1963) concerns a high school boy and girl whose first steps toward romance are ended when a bully forces them into a kissing game. It was a success at film festivals, and Verhoeven considers it to be his best student film and his first professional-looking product.

Upon completion of his university studies, Verhoeven was drafted into the military to serve a two-year stint (1964-66). Although initially posted to the Air Force to use his mathematics background to calculate rocket trajectories, Verhoeven was able to get himself reassigned to the Marine Film Service. There he made a documentary, *The Marine Corps* (*Het Korps Mariniers*, 1965), which was essentially a pro-military propaganda film celebrating the tercentenary of the Dutch Marine Corps. The film allowed Verhoeven to cut his teeth on directing action sequences, such as the one where hundreds of marines storm the beaches of Texel, a Dutch island. Verhoeven would use what he learned here when it came time to direct the battle scenes in *Soldier of Orange* and *Starship Troopers*. *The Marine Corps* was Verhoeven's first large-scale action film and his first movie in colour. It won first prize (the Silver Sun) at an international festival for military films.

Verhoeven left the Navy in 1966 intent on becoming a professional film director, but his plans were almost derailed when his girlfriend Martine got pregnant due to a torn condom. Verhoeven feared that he would have to give up his chosen profession, in which he was not likely to earn much money for a while, and take other jobs that would bring in enough income to support the baby. It was a time of great personal crisis, for abortion was still illegal in the Netherlands and the very thought of it brought on tremendous guilt. In fact, Verhoeven had a near-psychotic episode during a screening of *King Kong* (1933) when he thought the giant ape had been sent by God to punish him. On another day, a woman at a tram-stop gave him a leaflet advertising a Pentecostal church service which Verhoeven attended later that week. He became so caught up in the charismatic event that he believed he was getting messages from God and that his vocation was to be a preacher. However, as Verhoeven has said, "Even when I was emotionally moved, shaking and on the floor, and everyone around me was speaking in tongues, I felt fooled,"[28] for he came to realize that the woman who was translating the tongues for him into God's message about his future vocation was the same woman who first gave him the leaflet. He felt duped and manipulated as well as terrified that religious mania had brought him so close to psychosis.

ABOVE
Still from 'Let's Have a Party' (1963)
The school bully forces a blindfolded boy and girl into a kissing game. Afterwards, the girl runs off, furious.

LEFT
On the set of 'Let's Have a Party' (1963)
During the shoot, Verhoeven had to negotiate with 17-year-old Martine Tours to get extras for the film. She played the violin in the orchestra, and would later marry Verhoeven. Here Verhoeven is standing beside cinematographer Ferenc Kalman-Gall.

On the set of 'The Marine Corps' (1965)
Using the James Bond film 'Dr. No' as his inspiration, Verhoeven (left) staged the storming of the Dutch island of Texel. He was given many of the things he asked for, but he was not of sufficient rank to order the troops to attack during filming so he had to have higher-ranking intermediaries give the orders.

Still from 'Floris' (1969)
Floris van Rosemond (Rutger Hauer) returns to
the Low Countries in 1500 after a long time
away to find his castle being used as a toll house
by Marten van Rossum, flunky of Duke Karel
van Gelre. Floris fights for the return of his castle
and lands with the aid of Sindala, a magician he
met on his voyage around the world.

On the set of 'Floris' (1969)
When filming began on 15 July 1968, it was the first time a TV series of this size had been attempted in the Netherlands, so everybody in the production was learning by experience and doing a lot of improvising. Here a car with air let out of the tyres is being pushed (Verhoeven is the last man) to film Floris and Sindala (Jos Bergman) on horseback. The production went way over budget, but every gilder showed on the screen.

EXETER COLLEGE

LEARNING CENTRES

Verhoeven considers this mental crisis to have been directly responsible for his credo of extreme realism as a film-maker: "The effect this whole episode had on me was that, as an antidote, I started to film in a hyper-realistic way. My work became my anchor in reality."[29] Verhoeven also went on to explore potentially psychotic characters in his films, including Gerard (religious mania?) in *The Fourth Man*, Quaid ('schizoid embolism'?) in *Total Recall*, and Sebastian (God complex?) in *Hollow Man*. Verhoeven's moment of religious crisis is dramatized in *Spetters* when Maya takes the wheelchair-bound Rien to a Christian revivalist meeting, and Rien believes – just for a moment – that the faith healer has enabled him to walk. The manipulation of men's faith is seen in *Flesh+Blood* when Martin surreptitiously points a holy statue in the direction he wants his followers to go, which Verhoeven has called "a metaphor of how divine power is used by a human being to fulfil his own ambitions."[30]

Verhoeven's realistic approach to religion – provoked by his negative encounter with charismatic Christianity – would later lead him to join the Jesus Seminar, a group of progressive theologians who gather yearly to discuss the secular, historical roots of Christ, based on archaeological finds, recently discovered documents, and new translations of the Gospels. The scholars drop different-coloured beads into a box to show whether they think a New Testament passage about Jesus is authentic

(red bead), probably authentic (pink bead), could be true (grey bead), or definitely not authentic (black bead). Verhoeven, with his knowledge of both Latin and Greek, is the only layman member of the Jesus Seminar who is considered informed enough to vote with the governing panel. Verhoeven has said that if he were asked to vote on the question of Jesus' divinity or God's existence, he would probably cast a gray bead (for probably not) or a pink bead (for possibly): "I don't think we should be arrogant enough to say [Jesus] was also not God. It's not impossible. Even in physics, there's not much we can really be sure about. Materialism is only one way of looking at things."[31]

Verhoeven and Martine did have the abortion, freeing him up to pursue his career as a director. The next year (1967), the two entered into a marriage which has lasted to the present day, and they went on to have two daughters.

Verhoeven's next project was a television documentary about the leader of the Dutch fascist party before and during World War Two, *Portrait of Anton Adriaan Mussert* (1968). In researching the film, Verhoeven realized that as a boy he had actually witnessed the police leading Mussert through a crowd that had gathered to lynch him. Because Verhoeven's documentary was among the first to explore an unsavoury aspect of Dutch history – home-grown fascists and Nazi collaborators – the controversial program did not air until two years after it was completed.

Still from 'The Wrestler' (1970)
A young man has an affair with the wife of a bartender, who is also a fierce wrestler. The young man's father (Bernhard Droog) warns against the affair, but then the wrestler (Jon Bluming) thinks the father is having the affair.

Verhoeven would revisit the subject of home-grown fascism again – this time, American style – in *Starship Troopers*, a satire on a USA that has become a war-mongering dictatorship, with massed troops in thrall to their leaders, and heroes who wear Nazi uniforms and embody the Aryan "perfection" of Hitler Youth: "I was looking for chins and noses to match Leni Riefenstahl's vision of the ideal soldier"[32] in such pro-fascist films as *Triumph of the Will* (1935), Verhoeven has said.

After the Mussert documentary, Verhoeven turned to more light-hearted fare, a family-oriented television series, *Floris* (1968). This was a tongue-in-cheek swashbuckling adventure set in a romanticized Middle Ages, about a Dutch Ivanhoe or Robin Hood named Floris. In the first episode, Floris fights three bad guys at once with two swords. (It is interesting that, despite the show's comedic tone, some parents did complain about its violence. There would be many more such complaints about Verhoeven's future films!) Floris, a young nobleman, has a sidekick, Sindala, who brings the powers of Eastern magic to join forces with his master's sword fighting skills. For the part of Floris, Verhoeven cast a young unknown, Rutger Hauer, who was courageous and athletic enough to do his own stunts, including jumping off horses and diving from a castle turret into a moat. The collaboration with Hauer was the beginning of a long relationship which Verhoeven has described as a "non-sexual love affair,"[33] comparing their partnership to such actor-director pairings as Robert De Niro with Martin Scorsese and Marcello Mastroianni with Federico Fellini. After *Floris*, Hauer and Verhoeven would team up again for five feature films. *Floris* was also the first time that Verhoeven worked with writer Gerard Soeteman, who would go on to script all seven of the director's subsequent feature films made in the Netherlands. The most popular Dutch TV series in its day, *Floris* has since been rerun many times and has achieved cult status there. Following the success of *Floris*, Verhoeven had the idea of doing a less sanitized medieval drama, a *Floris* for adults. Seventeen years later, this would become the graphically realistic *Flesh+Blood* – also starring Rutger Hauer.

After the twelve 30-minute episodes of *Floris* for television, Verhoeven returned to cinema to make a short film called *The Wrestler* (*De Worstelaar*, 1970), a sex comedy about a father who tries to save his son from the consequences of the young man's adulterous affair with a wrestler's wife. The film is notable mainly for being the first of Verhoeven's collaborations with cinematographer Jan de Bont, who would go on to lens six of the director's future films, including *Flesh+Blood* and *Basic Instinct*, before becoming a successful director in his own right with such films as *Speed* (1994) and *Twister* (1996).

The Wrestler caught the eye of producer Rob Houwer, who wanted to make a sex comedy, *Business Is Business* (*Wat Zien Ik?*, 1971), based on a series of short vignettes about the lives of female prostitutes in Amsterdam's red-light district. The vignettes had been published as a wildly popular book by cabaret entertainer and television personality Albert Mol, who makes a brief but memorable appearance in the film as a blind date who takes a pastry in the face. (It was later revealed that Mol's stories had their source in tales he had heard about gay male encounters, which he had transposed into scenes of heterosexual prostitution.) It is interesting to note that despite Verhoeven's penchant for realistic depictions of sex in his later films, here he used stylization and humour to avoid offending audiences with overly graphic encounters between prostitutes and their clients. In critic Geoffrey Macnab's opinion, 'The cream-cake fights and kinky parlour games make for funny set-pieces, but they inevitably undermine the fitful attempts at social realism.'[34] Nevertheless,

Still from 'The Wrestler' (1970)
Marielle Fiolet plays the wrestler's wife, who is the object of desire. This short film was Verhoeven's first with cameraman Jan de Bont.

the film shows a moving solidarity between two female prostitutes, Greet and Nel, both of whom tire of the life and long for more permanent partners who will treat them with respect. The movie also satirizes the Dutch bourgeoisie, revealing the kinky underside and masochistic tendencies of supposedly proper and dominant middle-class men. Nel eventually escapes the abuses of her tawdry life for a boring but adoring middle-class husband. Although Nel is briefly tempted to return to her exciting life of prostitution, to be with her friends, she soon realises that she is glad to be out and embraces her new life.

Verhoeven directed *Business Is Business* not because this was the subject with which he wanted to make his feature-film debut, but because the opportunity presented itself as a way to break into the movie industry and he was afraid that if he didn't take it, there might not be another. When the film was completed, the distributor said it was so awful he regretted having agreed to play it. Producer Rob Houwer told Verhoeven that this would probably be his first and last movie. Yet, to everyone's great surprise, the film rode in on the tide of the sexual revolution just reaching the Netherlands and turned out to be a tremendous success, eventually becoming the fourth most popular Dutch film ever made. With the astounding popularity of his apprentice effort, Verhoeven was now ready to get more realistic about sex and to make what he considers to be his first true film, *Turkish Delight*.

ABOVE
Still from 'Business Is Business' (1971)
Albert Mol's book was supposedly based on female prostitutes he knew in Amsterdam's red-light district. In reality, many of the anecdotes came from gay men. Here a client dressed as a schoolboy (Allard van der Scheer) is cheeky with his 'teacher'.

LEFT
Still from 'Business Is Business' (1971)
This client (Henk Molenberg) likes to dress as a 19th-century maid and clean up all the mess.

OPPOSITE
Still from 'Business Is Business' (1971)
Jan Verhoeven (no relation to the director) plays a client who likes to dress as a chicken.

ABOVE
Still from 'Business Is Business' (1971)
When Nel (Sylvia de Leur) becomes disillusioned with her life as a prostitute she goes on a blind date, but the man (Albert Mol) is pompous so gets his just desserts.

RIGHT
Still from 'Business Is Business' (1971)
Blonde Greet (Ronny Bierman, right) goes to the opera with a married man (Piet Romer) but she becomes bored and cannot stand the stuffy atmosphere. She does not fit into this society, and recognising this she leaves the opera.

OPPOSITE
Still from 'Business Is Business' (1971)
Nel eventually marries a normal, boring, middle-class man, who has no idea that she was a prostitute.

LEFT
On the set of 'Business Is Business' (1971)
Verhoeven, here pausing to think whilst filming the wedding party, and screenwriter Gerard Soeteman had many doubts about the film because they wanted to make more important films.

BELOW
Queues at the cinema (1971)
After its premiere on 10 September 1971, over 2.3 million Dutch people went to see it out of a population of 13.3 million, making it the fourth most popular Dutch film of all time.

OPPOSITE
On the set of 'Business Is Business' (1971)
Cinematographer Jan de Bont films the chicken scene with Verhoeven, as ever, as close to the camera as he can be.

In the Netherlands 1973–1985

Turkish Delight (*Turks Fruit*) has been both popular and controversial since its premiere in 1973. Nominated for an Oscar as Best Foreign Film, it is still the highest-grossing Dutch movie ever made. It was even voted Best Dutch Film of the Century at the 1999 Netherlands Film Festival. Shot in a mere 42 days, the film was styled after those of the French New Wave, using mostly quick cuts, handheld camera, available light, no storyboarding, unrehearsed performances, and post-synched dialogue. The loose and improvised shooting style is effective in conveying the wild lust-for-life of the movie's artist-hero, Erik Vonk. This role marked Rutger Hauer's big-screen debut, proving his versatility in being able to play a randy bohemian sculptor – a far cry from his role as a medieval Dutch Ivanhoe in the family-oriented TV series *Floris*. This was also the first movie role for Monique van de Ven, who got the part after her screen test – as the heroine Olga dying of a brain tumour in the hospital – beat out the performances of more established actresses. To play this part in the film, van de Ven had to shave her head, and to show his support for her, cinematographer Jan de Bont also shaved his head. The two fell in love during the making of this picture and were married soon thereafter.

Opinion on the film remains sharply divided between those who consider it an artistic masterpiece and others who see it as trashy sexploitation. The film has been hailed as brilliant social satire and condemned as pornography. Something of a cross between *Love Story* (1970) and *Last Tango in Paris* (*Ultimo tango a Parigi*, 1972), the movie has been called a wonderfully satisfying romance, a beautiful and erotic film, the truest movie ever made about the 1970s sexual revolution, but it has also been attacked as sexist, obscene and nihilistic.

In a foreshadowing of the furore that would greet *Basic Instinct* twenty years later, women's groups protested the movie with pamphlets that read, 'The women and girls in this great film are all thumb-suckers and bitches' and 'Erik *can* be nice, but first you have to be very sick and die.'[35] Verhoeven's father, who had up to this point attended and praised all of his films, refused to see this movie because it contains Erik's blasphemous boast, "I fuck better than God!" Scenes of full-frontal nudity (male as well as female), cunnilingus and coitus, vomit and excrement (human and canine) brought on charges that the film had no other purpose than to shock audiences and was therefore merely repulsive and meaningless, like John Waters' *Pink Flamingos* (1972).

OPPOSITE
On the set of 'Flesh+Blood' (1985)
During his Dutch career, Paul Verhoeven considered Rutger Hauer his film alter ego, as Federico Fellini had Marcello Mastroianni and Francois Truffaut had Jean-Pierre Léaud.

PAGE 44
Still from 'Turkish Delight' (1973)
The film opens with Erik (Rutger Hauer) shooting Olga and her lover, and then strangling them. These shocking events are Erik's daydreams.

PAGE 45
Still from 'Turkish Delight' (1973)
Erik fucks a lot of women to overcome his heartbreak after his wife Olga leaves him. One woman asks for a souvenir from him and he draws the outline of his penis. He asks another what she thought of the sex and she replies that she did not feel God's presence. "I fuck better than God!" he tells her.

"Film in the teeth of the moralizing prejudices"
Paul Verhoeven

Still from 'Turkish Delight' (1973)
Erik and Olga (Monique van de Ven) first meet
when she gives him a lift home. They make love
in the car, but in the rush to get dressed Erik's
penis gets stuck in his zipper. He eventually
frees it using pliers, but then the car crashes.

*"Of course I want us to be indivisible and
immortal à la RoboCop but reality teaches the
opposite. From this dialectic I shoot my films: it
may look like pure provocation, but it is rage at
the insignificance of our design."*

Paul Verhoeven

Still from 'Turkish Delight' (1973)
Although they desire each other, each time Erik
and Olga try to make love there always seems to
be an interruption, or something bad happens.
Here, for example, after meeting for the first time
since the crash, both want to make love, but
Olga falls asleep sucking her thumb while
waiting for Erik to take a pee. Erik sits down and
watches her all night, captivated by her. Many of
their moments together are echoes of later,
darker events. The image of Olga upside-down
in the mirror is echoed when she is upside-down
during the brain scan. Erik's all-night vigil is
echoed when he stays up all night at Olga's
bedside as she lies dying in the hospital.

On one level, the film certainly has appeal as a tragicomic romance or bittersweet love story. In the beginning, Erik and Olga make love with a passionate intensity that is almost comical in its obsessiveness. No sooner has Olga picked up Erik as a hitchhiking stranger than they are having sex in the car, with the windshield-wiper spray doubling for his ejaculation. In another scene, a naked Olga leaps lustily on top of Erik in bed.

However, Erik's sensuality has a selfish side, and Olga eventually feels like a mere instrument to satisfy his desire: "The only thing you care about is fucking!" While Erik has idealized Olga as his muse, there is also a sense in which he is merely using her for his art, as when he sells a drawing of their lovemaking to a stranger, adding that once she is dead he will even sell her body to the hospital. When Olga leaves him for another man, Erik gradually learns her true value by being forced to suffer in her absence. First, he masturbates to exhaustion and physically falls apart. Then he has promiscuous sex with a series of women, none of whom compares to Olga. Finally, he slides into Olga while she is sleeping and, against her ensuing protests, rapes her in desperation.

It is only after being separated from Olga for a time that Erik is able to grow from selfish lust to compassionate love, symbolized by his nursing a seagull, injured by him, back to health and letting it fly free. Erik ultimately proves his maturity by loving Olga through the tragedy of her fatal illness, treating her to Turkish delight candy and buying a wig to cover her shaved head. Verhoeven had originally planned to end the film with Olga's soul going up to heaven, symbolized by white plane tracks in the sky, but the airline KLM would not oblige. Instead, we have a powerfully unsentimental ending in which Erik throws Olga's wig in the trash, showing that unlike before when he fell apart without her, he now has the strength to mourn her loss and move on to a new life.

On another level, we can also examine "the deeper theme of the movie" as Verhoeven has defined it: "love and death, Eros and Thanatos."[36] Erik and Olga's cheerful carnality shows a healthy appetite for life, as when he says that her sex tastes like oysters. The lovers attempt to embrace all aspects of bodily being; nothing physical is alien to them. Erik offers to lick Olga clean after she has been sitting on the toilet, and he is not afraid to search her stools to make sure there is no blood. Sticking a rose in Olga's rear end, Erik proclaims that only beautiful things can come from her. He accepts her body and soul, finding spiritual beauty within the flesh and not as something above or apart from it.

Against these life-affirming lovers are arrayed the deadly forces of bourgeois repression. Society wants this uninhibited couple to cover up, smothering their sensuality. This is conveyed symbolically when Erik's member is caught while he is zipping up his jeans after sex, and when the couple's car crashes while Erik is putting a fur coat on Olga. Olga's mother is repression personified, a hypocritical bourgeoisie who doesn't want her daughter to marry a bohemian artist, even as the mother herself is secretly committing adultery with a co-worker. The mother lost one breast to cancer, but she has made her daughter believe that she was responsible for sucking it off as an infant, thus instilling in Olga a lifelong fear of pregnancy and babies. This fear or "threat" that is "in her own head" becomes a tumour in Olga's brain, causing a change in her character where she decries Erik's lusty nature, cheats on him with another man, and then marries an accountant before surrendering to death from cancer.[37] The mother's bourgeois values of repression and hypocrisy *are* the cancer that infects Olga, turning her into a carbon copy of her prudish and

OPPOSITE TOP
Still from 'Turkish Delight' (1973)
There is a reason for every sex scene in the film, and each is filmed for a different purpose. Olga freaks out when her shit is red, because she fears she has cancer (her mother had breast cancer), but Erik explains that it is all the beets she had the previous night. Besides, he tells her, "Only beautiful things can come from your poopy-hole." To prove it, Erik puts a flower in her bottom and starts smacking it.

OPPOSITE BOTTOM LEFT
Still from 'Turkish Delight' (1973)
The couple get married on their own and go home to consummate the marriage, but they are constantly interrupted and eventually go to a big party given by Olga's parents.

OPPOSITE BOTTOM RIGHT
Still from 'Turkish Delight' (1973)
Olga is annoyed when Erik sells a picture of them making love. After they fight, they make up in the rain but once again they are interrupted. This time Olga is invited out by an old schoolfriend. At each stage, Olga is drawn back to her family and further away from Erik.

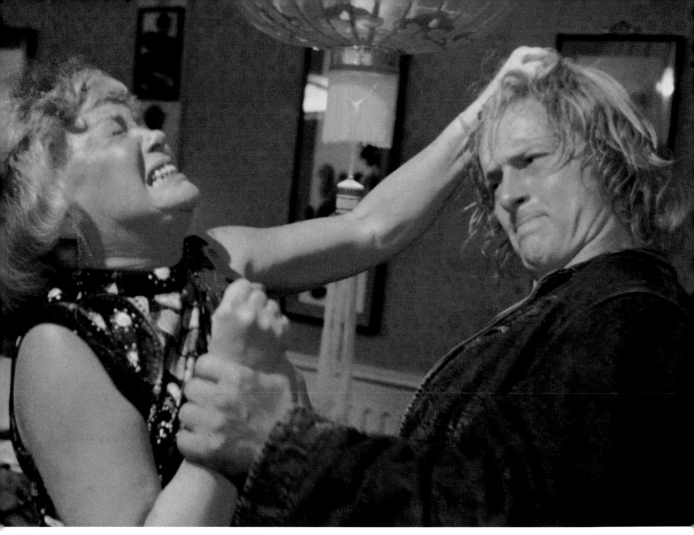

ABOVE
Still from 'Turkish Delight' (1973)
Things come to a head at a boorish family party, where Erik thinks Olga is cheating on him. He is repulsed by the behaviour of the family and friends and eventually throws up all over them. Here Erik and Olga's mother (Tonny Huurdeman), a hypocritical and cruel creature, fight at the end of the party. Olga decides to leave Erik.

RIGHT
On the set of 'Turkish Delight' (1973)
The production used a lot of hand-held camera work on many locations, which gave a fluidity and spontaneity to the film. Here the happy couple (riding in front of the man in the suit) go on a bike ride around Amsterdam after they are married.

prurient mother, making her pregnant with death. The scene where Erik vomits on both Olga and her mother as they sit next to the men with whom they are having affairs is not gratuitously repulsive or meaningless. It shows Erik's visceral disgust at their betrayal of love, their perversion of the body's natural desires into something sickening and shameful.

After the box-office success of *Turkish Delight*, Verhoeven was then entrusted with almost a million dollars to direct what was then the most expensive Dutch movie ever made, *Katie Tippel* (*Keetje Tippel*, 1975). The film was based on the memoirs of Neel Doff (1858-1942), a Dutchwoman who rose from rags to riches, working first as a prostitute ("Tippel" means streetwalker) and then as an artist's model before marrying a wealthy socialist. The film was originally to have given equal parts to Katie's life story and to the historical rise of socialism in Amsterdam in the late nineteenth century, but producer Rob Houwer cut the budget and scaled back the 500-page script, relegating politics to the background and reducing the grandeur of the film. It would now feature no epic scenes of steamboats or wealthy soirees, and it would include only a mini-version of a street clash between socialist demonstrators and police.

Still from 'Turkish Delight' (1973)
The harrowing conclusion shows Olga's mental deterioration from a brain tumour. Throughout the film, there have been examples of death being part of life and the idea that the universe is indifferent. The central characters know this yet make the best of it and have fun while they can. This is why Erik is able to live on after Olga's death.

"I feel very close in the way I'm expressing emotions to the composer Igor Stravinsky. His way of expressing emotions is not on the surface like Puccini. There is a distance and I personally love that. It gives the audience the possibility to look at everything through a dark mirror."

Paul Verhoeven

Still from 'Katie Tippel' (1975)
Based on the memoirs of Neel Doff, this film
shows her rise from the slums of Amsterdam up
through to the highest reaches of society. Here
Katie (Monique van de Ven) steals some bread
so that she and her family can eat.

Still from 'Katie Tippel' (1975)
Although Katie tries many jobs, each is
exploitative and demeaning in one way or
another. When Katie delivers hats to a house,
she finds out that it is a brothel, and that her
sister Mina (Hannah de Leeuwe) works there to
support the whole family. Here a client asks
Katie to lift her skirt as Mina masturbates on the
couch.

ABOVE
Still from 'Katie Tippel' (1975)
Whilst working late at night the milliner rapes
Katie, who loses her virginity.

RIGHT
Still from 'Katie Tippel' (1975)
Katie works at a tannery, where her hands are
burned by the vitriol. She leaves when the
manager wants to have sex with her.

However, what the film lost in scope, it gained in intimacy, and it could be
argued that the movie's political message is even stronger for being conveyed
through the person – and the body – of one woman. The state of grinding poverty
in which Katie and her family live is represented with graphic realism; we are given
an almost physical sense of their suffering. A drowning motif is established early on
when, after their rainy boat journey from the countryside to the city in search of
work, the family's basement hovel is flooded, drowning their puppy. At work in a
fabric-dyeing factory, Katie must plunge her hands into acidic water, making her
nails bleed. When a co-worker taunts her and steals her food, Katie forces the
woman's face into the acid bath. Later, after Katie has risen in the world and begun
spying on the poor for her bank-clerk lover, an angry woman plunges Katie's face
into a cup of hot chocolate, thus forcing Katie to face the fact that her new luxuries
have been purchased at the expense of others' continued poverty.

Like its socialism, the film's feminism is also conveyed physically – as something
felt and not just dictated to us. When we see the naked buttocks of a sailor rutting
on top of Katie's sister Mina, who has prostituted herself for some bacon, and when
we see Mina licking bacon off a plate while sitting on the toilet, the sexual
degradation of impoverished women is made nauseatingly apparent. Indeed, Mina is
presented as so immoral – using her whore's income to lord it over her family and
seeming to wallow in lust and gluttony – that the film risks blaming the victim. By
contrast, Katie's fall into prostitution is depicted with understanding and sympathy,
and portrayed through a motif of innocence violated. When Katie lifts her skirts for

a customer at a bordello who wants her because she looks innocent, there is an emphatic contrast between the old man's invading hand and her young legs. Later, when Katie is raped by her boss at a hat shop, the scene begins with her making playful shadows on the wall with her fingers – a play interrupted by the shadow of her employer's erect member, which he then forces on her, taking her virginity. After Katie's mother has pushed her into prostituting herself to a client, the mother goes to a butcher shop where meat is being cut – a symbol of the forced penetration that Katie's sex is suffering at that very moment.

Katie is thus presented as a victim who does what she must to survive, as when she gives her body to a doctor as the only way to get medicine so that she will not die of tuberculosis. As Verhoeven says, "Wherever she goes, her body is really her asset. She uses it, but mostly because she is abused and forced to use it."[38] That word "mostly" is interesting because some ambivalence toward Katie enters the film when she disowns her family, becomes the mistress of a bank clerk (Rutger Hauer), begins spying on the poor for him, and starts to dress up in rich finery. Is she now prostituting herself not for survival but for social advancement? Is she a struggling innocent or a hardhearted social climber and gold digger? (It is a curious fact that cinematographer Jan de Bont, now married to actress Monique van de Ven who plays Katie, would hiss at her from behind the camera, calling her a "slut" when she took off her clothes for sex scenes.) Katie eventually refuses to continue spying on the poor, and she leaves the bank clerk rather than commit adultery with him after he marries a rich woman. Moreover, Katie certainly prefers to earn money not as a

"In basic terms, Jost [Vacano] uses more blue and Jan [de Bont] uses more red. Jost's work has a more matter-of-fact quality, a sense of realism. Jan's [manner] is a little bit more [stylized] – it's a little more elegant, a bit warmer and more romantic."

Paul Verhoeven

ABOVE
Still from 'Katie Tippel' (1975)
When she becomes an artist's model, Katie begins to interact with a different social class and learns how to conduct herself in a way that is appropriate to her new class. Here Katie is enjoying a song and dance with bank clerk Hugo (Rutger Hauer), rich socialist Andre (Eddy Brugman) and painter George (Peter Faber).

RIGHT
Still from 'Katie Tippel' (1975)
Katie completely reinvents herself. This is demonstrated in the scene where she goes to a bath house, burns her old clothes, bathes and dons a new white dress and hat to meet Hugo. She then proceeds to act like the people who used to exploit her, by spying on businesses for Hugo, so that Hugo can make financial decisions about who gets and is denied money.

prostitute but as an artist's model and muse for a socialist painter, and she joins with the poor in a street march, which is where she again meets the rich socialist who marries her. Like Cinderella, Katie seems to be rewarded in the end for her suffering and for making the right moral decisions. Titles during the movie's closing moments tell us that "her indomitable spirit lives on in this film."

However, Verhoeven hints at some disturbing realism that might undermine the Cinderella myth. In the film's final scene, as Katie tends the rich socialist who has been grazed by a police bullet, we see her licking the blood from his wound, providing the merest suggestion of her as a vampire sucking away at his wealth. Originally, Verhoeven had planned to end the film with a further scene set several years in the future where Katie, now a rich woman, closes all her windows to shut out the screams of poor people begging in the streets. Earlier in the film, commenting on the money-grubbing, social-climbing bank clerk, Katie had said that "money turns people into bastards." The more realistic final scene, as originally intended by Verhoeven, would have shown Katie herself as having turned into one of these rich bastards.

Still from 'Katie Tippel' (1975)
In her new persona, Katie is no longer part of the family that made her a prostitute. When she says goodbye to them, her mother asks how they are to support the children. Katie says she should have fucked less, and has to kick her clinging mother away. As Katie says: "Money turns people into bastards."

"When I was in high school in Holland, there were already mixed-sex classes, because it's a progressive country. And I always felt that the women in my class were as interesting and intelligent as the men. So I really do feel that females are as important as males. And I like to see strong women – as strong as men, as intelligent as men, as resourceful as men."

Paul Verhoeven

ABOVE
Still from 'Soldier of Orange' (1977)
When Paul Verhoeven went to university at
Leiden in 1956, the initiation rites for the elite
student association included the head being
shaved and other humiliations. The film's central
characters are subjected to the same rituals.

RIGHT
Still from 'Soldier of Orange' (1977)
The naïve students before the onslaught of
World War Two: Alex (Derek de Lint), John
Weinberg (Huib Rooymans), Erik Lanshof
(Rutger Hauer), Guus LeJeune (Jeroen Krabbé),
Jack Ten Brinck (Dolf de Vries) and Nico (Lex
van Delden).

Still from 'Soldier of Orange' (1977)
The film was based on the dramatized memoirs of Erik Hazelhoff Roelfzema, a wealthy Leiden student who, during World War Two, had joined the Resistance, flown with the RAF and was eventually appointed aide to Queen Wilhelmina, who had fled to Britain with her government. However, the film is also imbued with the vivid memories of little Paul Verhoeven: explosions, body parts littering the floor, being forced to walk past the bodies of executed people.

Still from 'Soldier of Orange' (1977)
Erik and Guus join the Dutch army because they want to have an adventure, not because they believe in the fight.

On the set of 'Soldier of Orange' (1977)
This film gave Paul Verhoeven the opportunity to work on an epic story but time and money were not always available for him to film it on an epic scale, which brought him into conflict with producer Rob Houwer. This is a natural conflict, because the director wants the perfect film and the producer has to know when to say yes and when to say no. For example, in one scene, the script said ten planes, but Houwer could only supply two, and they could only make two passes within 20 minutes, so Verhoeven and his crew had to be ready for them!

After the budget cuts and downsizing of *Katie Tippel*, Verhoeven finally got to make an epic historical drama with *Soldier of Orange* (*Soldaat van Oranje*, 1977). At an eventual cost of $2.5 million, making it the most expensive Dutch movie at that time, this World War Two film featured large-scale action scenes of Nazi planes bombing and strafing the Netherlands. The film was Verhoeven's international breakthrough, prompting Steven Spielberg to invite him to Hollywood, where discussions with studio executives would later lead to a career in America. The film was also the first to bring star Rutger Hauer to international attention. Hauer plays a part based on the fictionalized memoirs of Erik Hazelhoff Roelfzema, whose path took him from college boy to Dutch Resistance fighter to aide de camp for the Queen. Hauer had been so convincing as a randy bohemian artist in *Turkish Delight* that Verhoeven at first thought he was wrong for the part of Erik, but screen tests proved that the actor could display a certain aristocratic bearing and confidence. *Soldier of Orange* was nominated for a Golden Globe Award as Best Foreign Film, and it is the movie that Verhoeven considers to be his favourite and his best from his Dutch period.

From one perspective, *Soldier of Orange* is Verhoeven's most conventional movie, an old-fashioned war picture with a rousing musical score, lots of action and intrigue, and a dashing hero who proves himself as a lover and a resistance leader. Erik gives up his seat on a seaplane to help his Jewish friend John escape to England;

On the set of 'Soldier of Orange' (1977)
Verhoeven's exuberance and drive are evident on all his films.

he rescues Robby from drowning; and he gets himself arrested so that Gus can evade capture. Erik's war adventure has him surviving a Nazi prison, going undercover to spy on the enemy, flying an RAF bomber, and returning victorious to the Netherlands as the Queen's adjutant. Involved in two love triangles, Erik gets the woman in each case, as Robby's fiancée Esther and Gus' girlfriend Susan gravitate toward Erik's bed. By contrast with the heroic Erik, the Nazis and their collaborators are demonized as they were in many of the movies made during and just after World War Two. SS officer Thelen is a cartoon caricature of impotent rage because he is unable to stop Erik from being smuggled aboard a ship while camouflaged by a crowd of drunken sailors. The Dutch Gestapo-man Breitner is both vicious and lecherous, groping his female aide and spying voyeuristically on Erik and Esther's lovemaking. Finally, there is Alex who abandons his Dutch friends to side with the Germans. After ignoring the pleas of a beggar boy and dropping a piece of bread in the mud, Alex meets a fittingly nasty end when he is blown up while sitting on an outhouse toilet.

If there is a boy's-adventure-tale aspect to *Soldier of Orange*, this is because Verhoeven was a boy when the Nazis invaded the Netherlands. He saw the war through the naïvely romantic eyes of a child: "For me war was a wonderful presentation of seeing rockets fly up, and planes bombing, or people being killed. I mean, I was seven, yeah? It was like living in an amazing movie."[39] However, some

Still from 'Soldier of Orange' (1977)
When a Resistance operation goes wrong Erik (in yellow coat) is picked up and sent to jail for interrogation.

boys grow up and become aware of what death is. As Verhoeven says, "Kids love violence. As an adult, you realize that violence is real. So my work is anchored in reality, it's hyper-realistic."[40] Throughout *Soldier of Orange*, Verhoeven has inserted scenes of harsh realism to undercut the romance of war and to challenge the simplistic division between heroes and villains.

Erik and his university friends may begin with the feeling that "a spot of war would be quite exciting" (more precisely, "a little bit of war is nicely suspenseful" in Dutch), but by the end four out of the six of them are dead, having suffered blows to the kidneys, bullets from a firing squad, anal torture, assassination for being a traitor and a beheading by guillotine. Most of Erik's heroic efforts can be seen as fatal failures. Despite his attempts to save them, both John and Gus are captured and killed. Erik's espionage efforts are not successful at smuggling out the Netherlands' future leaders; instead, they not only get more of his friends killed, they are also merely a diversionary tactic for the English and not some crucial contribution to winning the war.

Along with the results of their actions, Verhoeven causes us to question the character of these 'heroes'. The film begins with a fraternity hazing which strongly suggests that these college boys are already caught up in proto-fascistic rites of violence and humiliation. Erik's and Gus' love interest, Susan, walks over to a

ABOVE
Still from 'Soldier of Orange' (1977)
John is executed by the Germans. As the film
progresses, more of the friends are killed.

LEFT
On the set of 'Soldier of Orange' (1977)
Filming the jail sequence.

Still from 'Soldier of Orange' (1977)
In Britain, Guus and Erik are rivals for the affections of Susan (Susan Penhaligon). This is all part of their great adventure.

windowsill of dead and dying flies and crushes one with a pencil. Later, she rigs a game of chance so that Gus gets the more dangerous – and ultimately deadly – war assignment, leaving Erik alive to bed her. For his part, Erik reaches orgasm on top of Susan not by thinking of her, but by imagining the cities he is going to bomb. In Verhoeven's realistic view of things, love is contaminated by death, and virility is proven by violence.

At the same time, Verhoeven also holds out some hope for the future by suggesting that if heroes are fallible, villains are human, too. When Alex betrays his country to fight on the German side, it is at least in part because his mother, who is of German extraction, had been interned by the Dutch when the Germans invaded. Until the villainous bread-dropping scene near the end – which Verhoeven now regrets including in the film – Alex has been portrayed as a character of some dignity. (It is interesting to note that Verhoeven had originally considered the actor who plays Alex, Derek de Lint, for the role of Erik the hero.) Throughout the film, Erik and Alex retain their camaraderie even though they are fighting on opposite sides in the war. The two men even dance the tango together in a scene of homoerotic bonding modelled on the lesbian dance in Bertolucci's *The Conformist* (*Il conformista*, 1970). The ability of Erik and Alex to put friendship above politics, to remember their common humanity despite wartime differences, is a more

profoundly positive message than some stereotypical victory of good guys over "evil."

Gone, Gone (Voorbij, Voorbij, 1979), which Verhoeven made for Dutch television, is a kind of coda to Soldier of Orange, picking up on the lives of some Resistance fighters 35 years after the war. They have sworn to take vengeance on the Dutch SS man who shot their friend during the Resistance. However, when they happen upon the guilty party in the present, they discover that he is partially paralysed and decide to forgo his execution because he will suffer more by staying alive than if they kill him.

Still from 'Soldier of Orange' (1977)
When Erik sneaks back into the Netherlands as a spy, he meets Alex, now a member of the dreaded SS. Alex went over to the Germans because his German mother had been imprisoned by the Dutch, so his choice, although wrong, was human. Erik and Alex dance a tango, an erotic dance that hints at the homoerotic nature of the friendships between the students. The tango is also a stylised fight, showing how easily either man could have been fighting for the other side, and how easily the balance of power can change.

On the set of 'Soldier of Orange' (1977)
In an effort to escape to Britain in a merchant
ship, Erik and others pretend to be drunken
sailors. Here the choreography of the scene is
being rehearsed with Paul Verhoeven (right),
while Rutger Hauer (on the left in the back)
looks on.

On the set of 'Soldier of Orange' (1977)
Filming the scene, with Rutger Hauer falling over drunk.

Still from 'Gone, Gone' (1979)
The prologue shows members of the Resistance burying a comrade at the end of World War Two. The rest of this TV film follows them as they try to get revenge on the SS man who killed him.

Still from 'Spetters' (1980)
The film follows three young working-class friends who try to escape their blue-collar existence. They all have an interest in motocross racing and Rien (Hans van Tongeren) is the most gifted rider of the three.

As a change from the upper-class environment of university-educated men in *Soldier of Orange*, Verhoeven turned to the opposite end of the social spectrum to show us the struggling lives of working-class youths in *Spetters* (1980). The film's title, meaning 'spatters' of mud or grease, is also Dutch slang for 'hotshots' or 'hunks'. It is an ironic title because the three central characters are anything but 'cool'. A gritty depiction of the macho rivalry among three motorbike racing enthusiasts vying for success and being pursued by an opportunistic young woman, *Spetters* has scenes of masturbation, fellatio and homosexual gang rape that provoked considerable controversy. The first script was rejected by the government subsidy board, which refused to finance a film with such 'indecent' acts or with a heroine who was a 'whore'. Verhoeven had to submit a toned-down revision of the script before the film could be approved for funding, but he then went ahead and directed the original script anyway, making the board furious. Upon its release, critics tore into the film, denouncing it for giving a negative portrayal of Dutch society as decadent and perverted. A National Anti-*Spetters* Committee was formed, which picketed showings of the film and passed out flyers claiming that the movie was 'dangerous' in being anti-woman, anti-gay and anti-disabled.

A look at the film's sexually explicit scenes will help to determine whether they contribute to character development or are merely gratuitous shock tactics. The early scene where the three young men unzip and measure the length of their members certainly serves to establish their competition for male dominance. (It is

ABOVE
Still from 'Spetters' (1980)
The races provide an exciting and dynamic backdrop to the film, where one small mistake can make the difference between winning and losing. Here Rien passes Hans (Maarten Spanjer). Verhoeven chose the colour of the clothes according to the characters' personalities. Rien is in heroic white whilst Hans is in cowardly yellow.

LEFT
Still from 'Spetters' (1980)
The boys aspire to be like the champion Gerrit Witkamp (Rutger Hauer, left), who was modelled on the Dutch motocross rider Gerrit Wolsink. Here Rien wins the race, which will open up all sorts of financial possibilities for him.

interesting to note that Verhoeven actually made this scene less graphic than he had initially intended, for originally the youths competed to see who could climax first.)

Because Rien is the one of the three who shows the most promise as a future motocross champion, the woman Fientje takes up with him as a potential escape from her dead-end existence as a French-fry vendor. The scene where Fientje touches Rien's penis shows him at the height of his masculinity – he got the girl. However, this scene is also important in preparing for a contrast later on when, after Rien is paralyzed in a motorbike accident, Fientje leaves him because he is no longer a hot prospect, and the oral ministrations of his former girlfriend Maya are not enough to rouse him from impotence. Maya also brings Rien to a Christian revivalist meeting, but he is unable to rise from his wheelchair at the touch of the faith healer.

Verhoeven establishes Rien as a blue collar worker who sees his racing hobby as a way out of his impoverishment. However, the accident that breaks his body also crushes his dream of a rich life and his spirit. In the end, Rien rolls his wheelchair into the path of an oncoming truck. When the film was released, protestors booed Verhoeven on a talk show, claiming that his film encouraged disabled people to commit suicide for being useless. However, Verhoeven has shown attempts by Rien's girlfriend, parents, buddies, and nurses to help him survive his physical misfortune. It seems clear that it is Rien's overinvestment in his dream that leaves him with no reason for living.

After Rien, Fientje sets her sights on another boy in the group, Eef, who may have enough money to take her away to Canada. But Eef's money comes from beating up and robbing gay prostitutes. In one scene, Eef watches a hustler perform fellatio, then knees the man in the groin and steals his money. The explicitness of this scene is not gratuitous because Eef's voyeurism turns out to be as important as his violence: his gay bashing is a way of repressing his own homosexual desires. Earlier, in another graphic scene, Eef had remained soft, claiming drunkenness, despite a girlfriend's manipulations. This scene, too, becomes significant when we realize Eef's true orientation, as does the scene in which he and his buddies compared their members, which now takes on a homoerotic component. A culture of macho competition and his father's strict Calvinism both put pressure on Eef to deny his own homosexuality, but being gang-raped by the hustlers he has robbed forces him to recognize his true identity. Fientje's brother, who is one of the rapists, gets Eef to admit that he "liked it".

This theme of sexual self-discovery through violation is problematic and opens the film to charges of stereotyping gays as sadomasochists. Even if one argues that the barrier of repression in Eef was so strong it could only be overcome with violence, the idea that rape leads him to a healthy acceptance of his sexuality seems far-fetched and morally repugnant. When Eef goes on to establish a seemingly tender relationship with Fientje's brother, and when Eef's newly found self-acceptance gives him the courage to come out to his abusive father and to withstand another beating, this character growth seems almost too good to be true. Yet it is also possible to interpret Eef's character arc in quite a different way. Does he 'like' the male-on-male rape because his father's beatings have already instilled in him a penchant for masochistic enjoyment? Does his character spiral deeper into the cycle of male violence rather than finding a way out to health and self-acceptance?

The French-fry seller Fientje goes from Rien to Eef and eventually to the third friend, Hans, in an attempt to find a man who will free her from the hot, dirty work of a fast-food van. Some viewers have accused Verhoeven of misogyny in his

Still from 'Spetters' (1980)
After the accident that robs him of the use of his legs, Rien is persuaded to go to a revival meeting by his old girlfriend Maya (Marianne Boyer, right). For a moment, Rien believes that he has been healed and can walk again, but it is a false hope.

ABOVE
Still from 'Spetters' (1980)
When Rien becomes a successful motocross racer, Fientje (Renée Soutendijk) pursues him, and gets him a lucrative sponsorship deal.

LEFT
Still from 'Spetters' (1980)
Rien's disappointment in life is evident. His dream of a life racing bikes has been taken away from him after the accident, so he commits suicide.

ABOVE
Still from 'Spetters' (1980)
After Eef (Toon Agterberg, centre) beats up and robs homosexuals over a period of time, they get together and gang-rape him.

RIGHT
Still from 'Spetters' (1980)
It becomes clear that Eef's 'queer-bashing' arose from his confusion about his sexuality. He then begins a relationship with Jaap, Fientje's brother (Peter Tuinman, left), who was one of the men who raped him.

ABOVE
Still from 'Spetters' (1980)
Maya calls Fientje a "cunt with a cash register" because she seems to be only interested in money. However, Fientje feels she deserves the fur coat because she was the one who negotiated a big sponsorship deal for Rien, so she is being paid for the work she has done.

LEFT
Still from 'Spetters' (1980)
Fientje is the only one of Rien's friends who visits him after the accident, proving that she is not as cynical and uncaring as her reputation may suggest.

"The hero does not get a kingdom, but a chip shop and a girl with a (sexual) past. That does not mean to say she is not an acceptable match for a young man: it is real life. In our films, Paul and I have always resisted the odd idea that only romantic love can be real love."

Gerard Soeteman on 'Spetters'

On the set of 'Spetters' (1980)
Paul Verhoeven in action. With this film, his first
away from producer Rob Houwer, Verhoeven
had to prove himself able to stand on his own
two feet. The enormous stress was readily
apparent to everybody on the set during the
shoot.

portrayal of Fientje, arguing that she offers her body to men for her own economic
advancement and that she has no qualms about abandoning a man if he proves
unable to further her career. Is selling fries so bad that she must sell herself to escape
that life? After Fientje seduces the would-be champion Rien away from her, Maya
calls her "that greedy cunt" (or in Dutch, "a cunt with a cash register"). Indeed, we
see Fientje buying a fur coat, using some of the motorbike promotion money she
had prostituted herself to get for Rien. Her brother tells her that she likes it when
she has to give a blow job to a cop so that their fast-food van can park within the
city limits.

However, the fact that Fientje does not assent to her brother's comment and is
brushing her teeth after the sexual encounter suggests that there is another side to
her story. Verhoeven is careful to present her character with a well-rounded
ambiguity. Yes, she lusts after a fur coat, but she also looks longingly at a house, a
husband, and a baby. Yes, she abandons Rien after his accident, but she – unlike Eef
or Hans – at least goes to visit him in the hospital. She also plans to leave Hans
when he proves to have no future as a biker, but not before she checks to see that
he is unhurt after a fall. If the guys are in a macho competition to see who will be
the first to bed her, can we expect Fientje to behave with any more feeling toward
them and not to turn their sexual objectification of her to her own advantage? In the

end, Fientje does stay with Hans, and the two attempt to make a go of a disco bar that will also sell French fries. Verhoeven refuses to resolve our view of Fientje into some simplistic truth: she may be willing to settle for a small improvement and to settle down with a man she could someday love – or she may be using him as a mere stepping stone to her next opportunity.

On the set of 'Spetters' (1980)
Filming was intense and laborious. The cast and crew were often shooting continuously for 16 hours per day on locations away from home. In addition, the actors were young and inexperienced, so Verhoeven had to spend a lot of time coaching them.

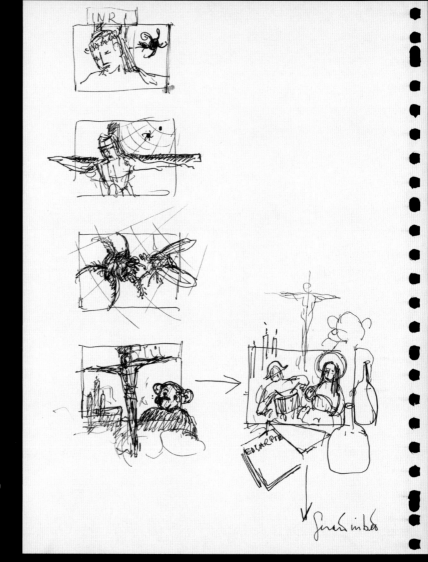

Storyboard for 'The Fourth Man' (1983)
Verhoeven draws extensive storyboards on his scripts so that he can plan how to tell the story visually. The title sequence shows a spider on a crucifix trapping and cocooning three flies caught in its web. As the camera tracks down the crucifix we see toys and religious memorabilia, including a Pietà, before we get a shot of the central character Gerard Reve.

Still from 'The Fourth Man' (1983)
Old drunk writer Gerard Reve (Jeroen Krabbé) wakes with the shakes in an image that ends the opening sequence. Verhoeven has introduced the themes that will dominate the film: the predatory spider and the fly; the compassionate Virgin Mary; the man on the cross; and the three victims.

Renée Soutendijk, who played Fientje, returned to play a similarly ambiguous role in Verhoeven's next film, *The Fourth Man* (*De Vierde Man*, 1983). Christine is either an innocent widow whose three husbands all just happened to die in unfortunate accidents, or she is a black widow who copulates with and then kills her mates. Gerard Reve (Jeroen Krabbé) is a gay, Catholic, alcoholic writer who fears that he will become the fourth man to be caught in her web, or he may be merely projecting onto her his own paranoid hallucinations about seductive and emasculating women. To sustain the uncertainty over whether Gerard's visions of Christine as a femme fatale reveal the truth about the danger he is in or are merely figments of his hyperactive imagination, Verhoeven combined elements from two pictorial traditions. For the colour and lighting, he used the Hyperrealism of Edward Hopper's paintings, which gave Gerard's eerie visions a razor-sharp clarity. For the symbolic content, he referred to 19th-century Symbolists like Franz von Stuck and Gustave Moreau. In addition, Verhoeven had symbolic colours and objects appear in both real and imagined scenes, further blurring the line between daylight and dream.

LEFT
Still from 'The Fourth Man' (1983)
Gerard dreams of strangling his annoying boyfriend with a bra at the beginning of the film.

ABOVE
Still from 'The Fourth Man' (1983)
Caught in Vlissingen after giving a talk, Gerard stays the night with widowed beautician Christine Halslag (Renée Soutendijk). He notices that she looks like his "beautiful boy" back home, and they make love.

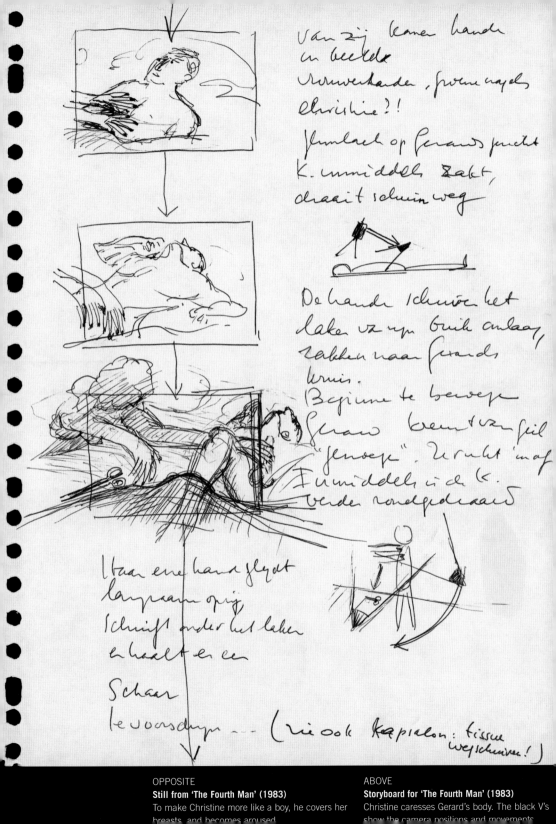

OPPOSITE
Still from 'The Fourth Man' (1983)
To make Christine more like a boy, he covers her
breasts, and becomes aroused

ABOVE
Storyboard for 'The Fourth Man' (1983)
Christine caresses Gerard's body. The black V's
show the camera positions and movements

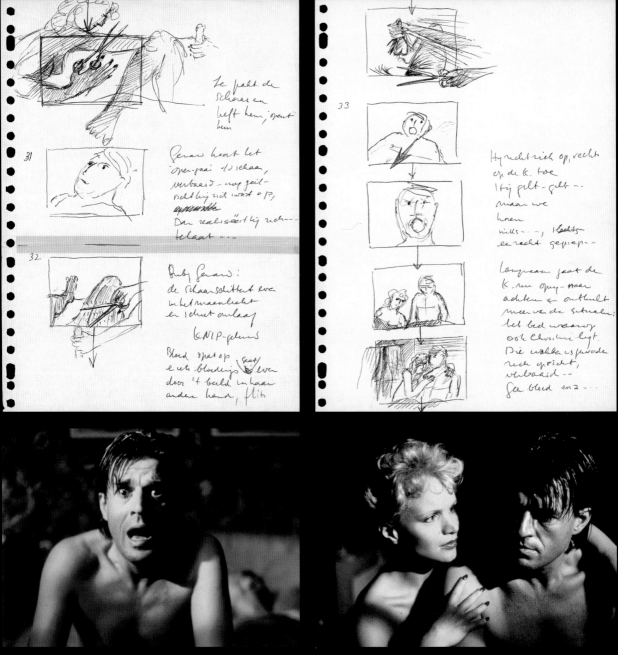

OPPOSITE TOP
Storyboards for 'The Fourth Man' (1983)
The scene is filmed almost exactly as it is
storyboarded. The only difference is that
sometimes the image is flipped to keep the logic
or story sense. For example, the severed penis is
held up with the left hand because the scissors
are held in the right hand.

OPPOSITE BOTTOM
Stills from 'The Fourth Man' (1983)
Christine cuts off Gerard's penis and Gerard
wakes up from his nightmare.

ABOVE
Still from 'The Fourth Man' (1983)
As well as the nightmares, Gerard also has
waking daymares. In this daymare the Virgin
Mary (Geert de Jong) shows Gerard a crypt
where three carcasses are being drained of
blood and a fourth urn remains to be filled.
Through these visions, Gerard begins to
understand that Christine, who has buried three
husbands, intends him to be the fourth man and
that he will die too.

On the set of 'The Fourth Man' (1983)
Verhoeven shouted abuse and argued with Jeroen Krabbé during filming to get the right state of depression and aggressiveness necessary for the part. Krabbé's character is always on edge, looking for opportunities (in this scene, to steal money from Christine), but at the same time afraid of the visions and warnings he is receiving.

In one scene, Gerard thinks he has awakened in bed from a nightmare only to find Christine castrating him with a pair of scissors – which turns out to be another nightmare. Verhoeven got the idea for this 'double awakening' from John Landis' *An American Werewolf in London* (1981). Other filmic inspirations for *The Fourth Man* and its surrealistic symbols include Bergman's *Through a Glass Darkly* (*Såsom i en spegel*, 1961, for the spider, schizophrenia and the occult) and the Dalí dream-sequence in Hitchcock's *Spellbound* (1945, for the eyes, and the key that looks like a gun). It is worth recalling that Verhoeven himself did some Surrealist painting while he was a student at the University of Leiden, including a painting of a naked *Woman Sitting* (*La Femme assise*) whose eerily enticing back is seen from behind, much as Christine's bare back is seen in the mirror by Gerard.

If we choose to believe Gerard's visions, all the signs do seem to point toward Christine as a kind of black widow. While the neon sign above her beauty salon is supposed to read 'SPHINX', a burned-out H and X (as in a witch's hex?) make it read as 'SPIN', which is Dutch for 'spider'. Did Christine seduce and slay her first three husbands in the same way that a spider catches and kills three flies during Gerard's vision at the beginning of the movie? Christine sells her own brand of cosmetics called Delilah, and she takes the scissors to his hair and then, in a nightmare, to his groin: is she planning to unman him as Delilah did Samson?

Gerard imagines a key that looks like a gun, which opens a door where three
hanging cow carcasses drip blood. This horrific hallucination finds its real-life
counterpart when a similar key opens a cabinet in which Gerard finds home movies
of Christine's three deceased husbands. Still later, Gerard and Herman, Christine's
boyfriend, open the door to a mausoleum where they find three urns with the ashes
of those dead husbands. Will Gerard or Herman be the fourth to die? One of the
husband's names was GE (compare GErard), and the other two were called HENK
and JOHAN (disturbingly similar to HErmAN). Christine has been filming Gerard
and Herman just as she did her former husbands, who are revealed in home movies
to have died from a parachuting accident (Christine mimes cutting the cord), a freak
lion attack (Christine growls and makes claws with her hands), and a boating mishap
(Christine scoops a dead fish from a tank). Then a fallen seagull, a lunging dog and a
drowned man all appear to Gerard as omens that he may be Christine's next victim.

However, the symbols pointing to Christine as evil are so numerous and they
interlock so ingeniously that they seem more like the products of psychosis than
psychic truths. Moreover, the film presents its terrors with a tongue-in-cheek tone,
as if poking fun at Gerard's outrageous fears. Certainly, the jokey and symbol-laden
The Fourth Man is quite different from the naturalistic, almost documentary style of
Verhoeven's previous films, and the director has admitted that he was having some

On the set of 'The Fourth Man' (1983)
As this scene develops, Gerard conveniently
discovers the photo of Herman (in red swimming
trunks) on Christine's desk. Verhoeven and
cinematographer Jan de Bont (at the camera)
film the looks and glances in such a way that we
know that Gerard stays with Christine because
he desires Herman. Christine's motives are
unknown, but she would have known of Gerard's
preference for boys from their lovemaking the
night before, and could have placed the photo in
view on purpose.

sport with critics who had attacked *Soldier of Orange* and *Spetters* for the superficiality of their characters. The many symbols do give depth to Gerard's character, but mostly in the sense of comically undermining his credibility as a seer of the truth. "I lie the truth until I no longer know whether something did or did not happen," admits Gerard at a lecture; "I project things onto [people] that don't exist."

I suggest that we take Gerard at his word. Consider how many of his nightmarish visions can be seen not as warnings about real danger, but as projections of his paranoid and guilty mind. Rich, androgynous Christine seduces Gerard and he later stays with her to get to her boyfriend, Herman, who is the real object of his desire. Gerard can only orgasm during sex with Christine by blotting out her femininity, covering her breasts and looking at her boyish bare back in the mirror. Later, he comments on the similarity between Christine's and Herman's nude backs. Then, in the beach scene where Christine cannot feel the piece of glass she has lain on because of a numb spot on her back, Gerard takes this lack of sensitivity as a sign that she is a witch. But it is he who has been insensitive to her, and he who fears supernatural retribution on her part for how he has mistreated her.

In another scene, Gerard masturbates while peering through a hole in a door at Herman's buttocks thrusting into Christine. This image of the eye recurs in his nightmare vision, when a bloody eye – like his own spying one – pushes through a hole in a door, and Herman appears with one eye hanging out, as later an iron rod will be driven through his eye. If thine eye offend thee, pluck it out – or rather, be afraid that a vengeful Christine will put it out. In the scene where Gerard gazes at Christine's photo of hunky Herman in a red swimsuit, Gerard thinks, 'I've got to have you even if it kills me.'

When Gerard climaxes during sex with Christine, he cries out, "through Mary to Jesus", and later he imagines that a life-sized statue of Jesus on the Cross turns into Herman hanging there in his red swimsuit. Christine is not loved for herself, but as a means to Herman; Gerard doesn't want her, but her man. But his guilt over such misogyny and blasphemy becomes a fear of persecution. Gerard imagines pulling down the swimsuit of Herman on the Cross so that he can get at the boy's genitals, even as later Herman pulls down Gerard's trousers to fellate him, but it is at this very moment – the attainment of his desire for Herman – that Gerard sees the urns containing the ashes of Christine's former husbands. At some level, Gerard knows that he has committed a deadly sin by seducing Christine to steal her boyfriend, and somewhere in his mind he has sentenced himself to death. Caught in his own web of deceit and desire, Gerard is the black widow he fears.

"We know from the beginning that [Gerard] is a Roman-Catholic and that he is homosexual. So when he is expressing his fantasies, it's normal for this character to combine both things and see a homosexual Christ."

Paul Verhoeven

OPPOSITE
Still from 'The Fourth Man' (1983)
As Gerard becomes more manic he imagines Herman (Thom Hoffman) on the cross and starts to pull down the trunks when he is disturbed by an old lady.

ABOVE
Still from 'The Fourth Man' (1983)
Finally, Gerard traps Herman in a mausoleum. When they start to make love Gerard sees that

Still from 'Flesh+Blood' (1985)
The film opens with Arnolfini (Fernando Hilbeck, second left) promising Hawkwood (Jack Thompson, left) and his mercenaries (including Orbec (Bruno Kirby), Cardinal (Ronald Lacey), Karsthans (Brion James) and Martin (Rutger Hauer)) the spoils of victory if they can get his city back from the enemy.

After years of having to struggle to secure funds for his movies from the Dutch government subsidy board, which wanted to produce films on less controversial subjects, Verhoeven decided to seek money elsewhere for his next project, *Flesh+Blood* (1985), whose title alone announced that it would be dealing with sex and violence. (Its original title, *God's Own Butchers*, was hardly less controversial.) At this point in his career, Verhoeven wanted to make movies with American money for the American market without having to move to America, because he did not want to lose touch with his native European culture. When he was able to obtain most of the film's $7.5 million budget from a Hollywood studio (Orion) while also being allowed to remain in Europe (Spain) to make the movie, Verhoeven seemed to have gotten the best of both worlds.

However, the dream-come-true soon turned into a nightmare.

Verhoeven had originally planned for the film to centre on two old friends who become rivals, much like Robert Ryan and William Holden in *The Wild Bunch* (1969). Hawkwood and Martin are both members of a medieval band of mercenaries who are promised the spoils of victory if they help a nobleman, Arnolfini, take back his city from the enemy. But once the battle has been won, Arnolfini breaks his promise, depriving the band of their loot and driving them from the city. To get a country house so that he can retire from soldiering, Hawkwood sides with Arnolfini against his own former band and is later forced to lead a posse in pursuit of his friend Martin, who has kidnapped Agnes, the bride betrothed to

Still from 'Flesh+Blood' (1985)
Karsthans and Martin maim and kill everybody they can. However, Arnolfini reneges on his promise and pledges land to Hawkwood if he rids the city of the mercenaries.

Arnolfini's son. This was Verhoeven's intended story, but the Hollywood studio had other plans. Orion thought the film needed a love interest, and so the character of Agnes was brought to the foreground and the movie became about the way she is torn between Martin, her kidnapper, and Steven, Arnolfini's son and her would-be saviour. Verhoeven came to regret giving in to the studio on this demand: "The triangular relationship Martin-Agnes-Steven is now the main story line, but in retrospect I think we should have stuck with Hawkwood and Martin. The failure of *Flesh+Blood* was a lesson for me: never again compromise on the main story line of a script."[41]

In addition to Hollywood money and interference, Verhoeven also received funding from Spanish, Dutch and other sources, each of whom wanted to impose their own ideas, technicians and actors. As with most international co-productions, Verhoeven cast actors from various countries in what seemed like a smart appeal to the worldwide market, but trying to direct American, Dutch, British and Australian performers, while working with a crew who had diverse customs and languages, was fraught with frustrating delays and aggravating disagreements. Faced with their drinking, drugs and early disappearances from the set to go party on the beach, Verhoeven sometimes felt that his cast and crew were themselves a band of mercenaries mutinying against him as their leader. The shoot grew so chaotic that at one point Verhoeven feared he would be fired by the studio and replaced by another director.

BELMONTE CASTLE: before reconstruction

BELMONTE CASTLE: reconstruction design

Trouble also came from a most unexpected quarter, actor Rutger Hauer, with whom Verhoeven had always worked so well in the past. Hauer had been acting in Hollywood films for a few years, most notably as a vengeful android in *Blade Runner* (1982), and he was determined to get rid of his image as a villain in order to obtain more leading roles as a hero. Hauer was also just wrapping up work on *Ladyhawke* (1985), a medieval fantasy adventure where he played a valiant knight the audience can identify with and root for. It was this kind of traditional hero that Hauer wanted to play in *Flesh+Blood*, but Verhoeven did not intend to make just another medieval fantasy or sword-and-sorcery adventure. Instead, he wanted to inject some realism into the myth, to make a counter-fairytale about the true Middle Ages, which he saw as "a cruel, wanton, dangerous, stinking time in which to live."[42] As Martin, Hauer was expected to play a complex character who, though he aspires to higher things, begins as a rapist and a marauder. "We thought that the mixture of good and evil made [the characters] more convincing, more true,"[43] explains Verhoeven. But this mixture also meant that Hauer would not get to play the chivalrous, gallant, decent hero that would be good for his Hollywood career. He and Verhoeven fought so bitterly over the nature of this role that their long-term friendship was ruined and they have never worked together again. There is a sense in which Hauer had the last laugh because *Flesh+Blood*, with no hero to root for and no happy fantasy element to lighten its unpleasantly realistic depiction of the Middle Ages, bombed at the American box office.

Nevertheless, it is the moral ambiguity of its characters and the tough-minded integrity of its historical representation that have made *Flesh+Blood* a critical and cult favourite. On the one hand, Martin and his mercenary band are greedy, murderous, lustful, gluttonous and superstitious – prone to all the weaknesses of the flesh and the follies of ignorance. A defrocked priest called the Cardinal has the group go in whatever direction is pointed to by a supposedly holy statue of Saint Martin – a statue which Martin (Hauer) is manipulating to suit his own selfish ends. The Cardinal enforces 'Christianity' with a sword, using it to put to death any non-believer who dares to challenge the divinity of the statue. On the other hand, the band of mercenaries and their whores are humanized in their physical suffering and their sympathetic bond with one another. Arnolfini plays a dirty trick on them when he breaks his promise, exiling them from the city without their reward for winning the battle. Having risked their lives for the nobleman, what had the group to look forward to besides the physical pleasures of food, drink and fine things? Unlike Arnolfini, who exercises his hierarchical power to keep the loot for himself, the mercenary band has a communal practice of share and share alike. We sympathize with the pregnant prostitute Celine's need to bond with Martin as her one and only man, and we suffer with her when she screams in labour and then grieves over the death of her stillborn baby. One of the most poignant scenes in the film occurs when Miel, after losing his male companion Orbec to the plague, throws himself on his own sword to join his lover in death. There are thus many ways in which the mercenaries seem superior to their supposedly noble betters.

No wonder Agnes (Jennifer Jason Leigh) has so much trouble choosing between the mercenary Martin and the nobleman's son, Steven. After learning about sex from her maid whom she watches making love to a soldier, Agnes meets her bridegroom Steven, but he disappoints her by claiming that a wife would only distract him from his books and scientific studies. Yet she perseveres and, like Eve tasting the apple and then tempting Adam, Agnes eats from a mandrake root and gives Steven a bite,

ABOVE
Costume design for 'Flesh+Blood' (1985)
This costume was used by Martin at the end of the film (see page 92). Although a lot of research was done for the film, and the medieval period was a favourite subject for Verhoeven, in retrospect he made a mistake in not drawing visual storyboards because he had wanted a looser visual approach. This meant that he had to improvise with a large cast, many extras, horses, equipment and locations.

OPPOSITE
Production design for 'Flesh+Blood' (1985)
Belmonte Castle was one of four major locations used in Spain. It had been used for Anthony Mann's epic film 'El Cid' (1961), which starred Charlton Heston and Sophia Loren.

ABOVE
Still from 'Flesh+Blood' (1985)
The central conflict between Arnolfini's son Steven (Tom Burlinson) and Martin is a conflict between science (Steven is a Renaissance man) and superstition (Martin uses the Cardinal and a religious figure to control his mercenaries). In this scene Hawkwood contracts the plague from the little girl, but Steven cures him using his scientific knowledge.

RIGHT
Still from 'Flesh+Blood' (1985)
In this romantic scene, Steven is prompted by Agnes (Jennifer Jason Leigh), his naïve bride-to-be, to eat a mandrake so that they fall in love. They ignore the hanged men, the men whose ejaculation at the moment of death produced the semen that grew into the mandrake. This is also a challenge to Steven's scientific way of thinking.

insisting that they will now love each other forever. This is a rather romantic scene, but the fact that it occurs beneath the hanging corpse of a man whom they both ignore – a man whose ejaculation at the moment of death produced the semen that grew into mandrake – suggests that Steven's and Agnes' romance is built on a repression of the physical. It is an idealization with no true understanding of bodily desire or death.

Where Steven is romantic and repressed, Martin is physical to the point of being animalistic. After kidnapping Agnes, he rapes her, exclaiming, "Let's see if this angel bleeds." Martin is both satisfying his lust and using his sex as a weapon to take by force the angel or noblewoman who would otherwise be beyond his reach as too good for him. But Agnes surprises him, countering his bid for power over her by saying, "You won't get me to scream. If you think you're hurting me, you're wrong. ... I *like* it! ... *I'll* take *you*!" – a statement which prompts the other mercenaries who are watching the rape to comment, "Hey, Martin, *she's* fucking *you*." Agnes' motives here are complex. On one level, she is a sexual novice merely repeating the words she heard her maid use with the soldier. Also, as she will do again in later scenes, she is claiming to like sex with Martin in the hope – which proves successful – that he will bond with her and not allow the other men to rape her. In addition, there may be proto-feminist defiance in her statement, a refusal to give him the

ABOVE
Still from 'Flesh+Blood' (1985)
Martin and his band kidnap Agnes for revenge
and take over a castle. Agnes sleeps with Martin
so that he will protect her, and in the process
changes him.

LEFT
Still from 'Flesh+Blood' (1985)
Agnes is sexually inexperienced but soon learns
to use her body to help her survive.

Still from 'Flesh+Blood' (1985)
The final showdown between Steven and Martin.

satisfaction of believing that she is his victim. However, there is also the politically incorrect possibility – here but more particularly in the later sex-in-the-bath scene between Martin and Agnes where the line between coercion and consent is blurred – that she is responding to his physicality. In the bath scene, Agnes grabs Martin's penis, getting the better of him, and then says, expressing her sexual curiosity (and desire?), "I can feel it. I want to see it." As Martin caresses her breasts, commenting on the softness of her skin, Agnes asks him whether the other women he has been with had soft skin like hers, as if she were jealous. In the dinner banquet scene, Agnes teases Martin's crotch with her foot under the table, while sensually eating food with her fingers like he does, echoing the erotic dining scene from *Tom Jones* (1963).

If Agnes discovers her sexuality through Martin, he is in turn ennobled by her. She teaches him to eat with a knife and fork; she gets him to wear white rather than the dirty red of lust and violence; and she has him establish an emotional bond with her to the point where he saves her several times from being raped by other men. However, Martin is never ennobled to the extent of recognizing her rights as a person separate from himself. When he fears that she might choose Steven over him, Martin covers Agnes' face with gauzy bed-curtains like an ironic bridal veil and, in a scene inspired by *Othello*, attempts to strangle her. Unable to rise above his strongly but wholly physical connection to Agnes – "You're in my blood" – Martin would rather kill her than see her go with another man. In the end, Steven saves Agnes from Martin, and she leaves the castle with the romantic but repressed nobleman – but not without a regretful look back at Martin, the man who wanted her with such murderous desire.

Flesh+Blood did poorly at the US box office. Verhoeven has speculated that without realizing it, he had made a film that was too cynical and downbeat for an American audience. In the end he concluded that as much as he loathed leaving his native Netherlands culture, he would have to go live in America if he wanted to make American films. Only by immersing himself in the USA could he hope to understand American tastes and attitudes. Moreover, making movies in the Netherlands had become increasingly difficult, given the public protests and bad press for films like *Spetters* and the government's reluctance to fund Verhoeven's kind of controversial cinema. As Verhoeven was at the airport about to leave for Hollywood, his parting words were caught by a camera crew who were ironically filming a documentary about the bright future of Dutch movie-making: "At the moment there is too much negative feedback about my work in the Netherlands. You waste so much time and energy setting up a film in the teeth of the moralizing prejudices of all the committees you have to face in this country in order to get your money."[44] In a later interview, Verhoeven explained that "One of the reasons I left the country was that the government subsidy board wasn't willing to give me any money because they thought that I was an indecent, perverted, decadent person. Which is probably true, but they shouldn't have held it against me."[45]

And so in September 1985 at the age of forty-seven, Verhoeven flew from the Netherlands, where he was famous, to Hollywood, where he was virtually unknown, and attempted to make it as a mainstream director in the cinema capital of the world.

ABOVE
On the set of 'Flesh+Blood' (1985)
Verhoeven: "It was agony all the way. What a mess! I have never felt so unhappy as with 'Flesh+Blood'. It just made me livid if something did not work - and hardly anything did. The computer in my head became completely overloaded."

LEFT
On the set of 'Flesh+Blood' (1985)
Although Rutger Hauer is imprisoned, the hand poking out from under his shirt shows that the tied arms are fake. During the making of the film relations between Verhoeven and Hauer deteriorated to such an extent that they have not worked together since.

In Hollywood
1985 to the Present

Verhoeven's first break in Hollywood came with the opportunity to direct an episode of the HBO cable TV series, *The Hitchhiker*. Entitled 'The Last Scene' (1986), the show was about a director who threatens his female lead to get her into the right mood for a horror movie. However, in the last scene, *she* turns the tables on *him*. The story suited Verhoeven's liking for strong, intelligent, resourceful women, but the main reason he took the job was to test whether or not he was able to direct an American crew. He was.

In fact, Verhoeven would soon gain a reputation for being unusually open to collaboration with his crew, and for working closely with actors to bring out their best performances. As producer Alan Marshall has said, "I think he's very kind on actors. I think he's wonderful on actors. He cajoles them into a performance."[46] According to Elisabeth Shue (*Hollow Man*), "I respect [Verhoeven] for his obsession and his passionate vision. He is only intense because he cares. He's respectful of the people he works with; he *loves* to make movies."[47] And Michael Ironside (*Total Recall, Starship Troopers*) has commented, "I think if Paul told me to sit in the corner on my head and spit nickels, I could do it."[48]

When Verhoeven first got the script for what was to become his next film, *RoboCop* (1987), he threw it across the room after reading only twenty pages, dismissing it as just another formulaic sci-fi actioner. However, his wife Martine retrieved it from the trash and convinced him that the story had more layers than that, including terrific potential as a satire on Reaganomics and corporate greed. Verhoeven also figured that a genre film with lots of action and little dialogue (English was still problematic for the Dutch director) would not be a bad choice for his first movie made in the USA, and indeed *RoboCop* would become his breakthrough American film. Budgeted at $13 million – not much money at the time but almost twice as much as Verhoeven had ever had to work with – *RoboCop* became the sleeper hit of summer 1987, shooting up to number one on *Variety*'s Movie Top Ten list, making $55 million at the US box office during its first year of release, and then doubling that in its next year on the international market. The film inspired two movie sequels and a TV series, and the character of RoboCop became a pop icon, spawning merchandising tie-ins that included dolls, T-shirts, video games and pinball machines.

Still from 'RoboCop' (1987)
This is the story of a man in search of his identity. He is an American Jesus with a gun, who is crucified and then resurrected, and kills rather than arrests.

"You can do a comic-book movie and still put your soul into it"

Paul Verhoeven

95

ABOVE
On the set of 'RoboCop' (1987)
Murphy is shot repeatedly by Clarence
Boddicker and his gang. For some of the shots
that showed the horror of bullet wounds, Rob
Bottin created special life-size puppets. These
would require one or more operators to make
them move. This torso capable of facial and
body movement was used for the bullet to
Murphy's head.

RIGHT
Storyboard for 'RoboCop' (1987)
Verhoeven draws a schematic of where each
character is in relation to Murphy, the cop they
are shooting. Verhoeven said that he wanted to
"show a crucifixion, as if Satan kills Jesus".

ABOVE
Still from 'RoboCop' (1987)
When Emil Antonowsky (Paul McCrane) is
covered in toxic waste, his body starts to melt.

LEFT
On the set of 'RoboCop' (1987)
Stephan Dupuis and Bart Mixon apply make-up
designed and created by Rob Bottin.

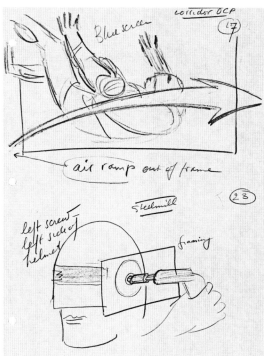

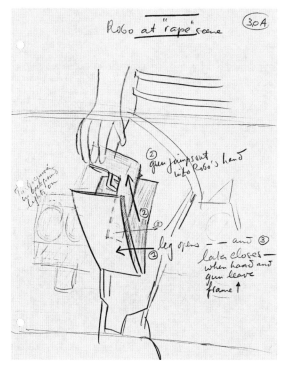

Writer Ed Neumeier got the idea for a robot who's also a cop from *Blade Runner*, with its policeman hero (Harrison Ford) tracking androids while he himself may be one. The machine-man played by Arnold Schwarzenegger in *The Terminator* (1984) was also an inspiration, and in fact Schwarzenegger was considered for the role of RoboCop, but the RoboCop suit was so bulky that when placed on top of the former bodybuilder's muscles, it would have ended up making him look like the Pillsbury doughboy. (However, Schwarzenegger did star in Verhoeven's next film, *Total Recall*.) Influenced by the look of the female robot in Fritz Lang's silent sci-fi classic *Metropolis* (1927), the RoboCop suit cost $600,000 and took six months for designer Rob Bottin to create. The Robo suit was not an immediate success with actor Peter Weller, who was so disappointed with its heaviness and clunkiness that he refused to wear it, arguing that it made him look foolish, like Gort in *The Day the Earth Stood Still* (1951). Producer Jon Davison actually fired Weller from the production, but this was really just to galvanize the actor into coming back to work. Since the suit had been sculpted to fit Weller's body, there was really no possibility of any other actor playing the part. Consulting a mime, Weller found a way to make the weight of the suit work *for* him, adding pathos to the RoboCop character by using body movements like those of Boris Karloff's monster in *Frankenstein* (1931). Each day it would take Weller two to three hours to be fitted into the RoboCop suit (although it took nine hours the first time), and he would lose three to four pounds of weight from perspiration, needing constant rehydration. In the end, Weller, who is

ABOVE
Still from 'RoboCop' (1987)
More machine than man, the suit that Peter Weller wears was designed by Rob Bottin and inspired by the robot in 'Metropolis' (1927). A mime coach helped Weller develop his distinctive movements in the suit, like turning the head and body separately.

OPPOSITE TOP
Still from 'RoboCop' (1987)
RoboCop's imposing shadow dwarfs the rapists. RoboCop has to clean up Old Detroit so that OCP can build Delta City (as per the billboard).

OPPOSITE BOTTOM
Storyboards for 'RoboCop' (1987)
Some of Paul Verhoeven's ideas for RoboCop, including the framing when the helmet is removed at the steel mill (see page 104). Also shown is the mechanism for the gun coming out at the rape scene: 1) The leg opens. 2) The gun jumps into the hand. 3) The leg closes. When RoboCop twirls the gun before he replaces it (like TJ Laser, the TV cop that Murphy's son liked), we know that Murphy is still alive somewhere under this sad, metallic creature.

a Method actor, became so bonded to the character that he would insist on being addressed as "Robo" whenever he was in the suit.

If RoboCop is technology with a human face, his nemesis – E(nforcement) D(roid)-209 – is a soulless, lethal machine. While RoboCop is in fact a man in a suit, ED-209 is an artificially animated thing. To create the special effect that is ED-209, Verhoeven blends together shots of a large, live-action version with those of a smaller model. The big ED-209 – seven feet tall and weighing three hundred pounds – is filmed from below to make him look even more immense, towering over his prey, dominating the competition. This live-action version is seamlessly intercut with a puppet-sized model, which is stop-motion animated like the monsters in Ray Harryhausen films, making ED-209 move with a decidedly inhuman deadliness during his scenes of mechanized man-slaughter. Designer Phil Tippett took care that ED-209 would not look cute, but hard and mean, like a cross between a killer whale and a US Air Force jet. In a reference to US violence in Vietnam, ED-209 was also modelled after a Huey helicopter. In the film, the enforcement droid is introduced by a scientist named McNamara (after Nixon's Secretary of War) and described as having been designed for "urban pacification" (a euphemism common during the Vietnam War). Exhibiting the redundancy (*four* hydraulic rams on his legs) and stupidity (an open grill area for his 'mouth') of too many corporate products, ED-209 malfunctions, machine-gunning a junior executive during a boardroom demonstration, and fails at performing certain basic tasks which humans can easily do, such as walking down stairs. However, as a corporate VP says, "I had a guaranteed military sale with ED-209. ...Who cares if it works or not!" The satire of

Stills from 'RoboCop' (1987)
RoboCop is busy on his first night. He stops a liquor store hold-up (opposite top), a gas station hold-up (opposite bottom left), dispatches some rapists (page 98) and disarms a hostage situation (above). Verhoeven and editor Frank Urioste cut this together so quickly (Verhoeven prefers things to happen in real time) that it is easy to miss the ironic signs in the production design. The 'SHELL' sign becomes 'HELL' (opposite bottom left) and the sign above the store doorway reads: 'Made the American Way' (opposite bottom right).

Still from 'RoboCop' (1987)

Dick Jones (Ronny Cox) introduces the ED-209 ("the future of law enforcement") to the OCP board. The corporation want to replace cops with this robot and also sell it to the military.

"The big problems are in the American social structure: crime, drugs, the urban environment, poverty, lack of education, and the availability of guns. The politicians don't deal too much with those problems; it is easier to blame Hollywood for causing decadence in American society."

Paul Verhoeven

ED-209 as an example of corporate threat and overkill continues through the end of the film's closing credits, which conclude with the warning that 'This motion picture is protected under the laws of the United States and other countries and its unauthorized duplication, distribution or exhibition may result in civil liability and criminal prosecution by enforcement droids.'

To avoid an X rating, which would have made the film unplayable in most cinemas, Verhoeven had to submit *RoboCop* to the MPAA eight times, cutting back on the violence each time. Ironically, the director has argued that the original version (now available on DVD) might actually be less disturbing because its violence is so over the top that it is funny in a comic-book or cartoonish way. The X-rated overhead shot of a junior executive's body being jerked around on a table as it is riddled with bullets is such overkill that it might be viewed as comic carnage. However, the scene where Murphy (Peter Weller), the human cop with whom we identify as the hero, has his hand shot off and his body blown apart bit by bit is horrifying and tragic, especially in its X-rated version. This brutal, bloody scene is excruciatingly extended. Its ultra-realistic violence forces us to feel what bullets do when they rip through human flesh. Here is Verhoeven taking the sci-fi action genre, with its fake violence that looks as though it would be fun to imitate, and adding some nasty, nauseating violence – closer to that of the Vietnam War – that is

ABOVE
Still from 'RoboCop' (1987)
Jones tests the ED-209 on one of the OCP
executives.

LEFT
On the set of 'RoboCop' (1987)
Unfortunately, the ED-209 malfunctions and kills
the OCP executive. Jones cannot understand
why they should scrap the robot because they
have sold things before that do not work.
Verhoeven and the writers are satirizing the
'Greed is Good' corporate mentality that prevails
to this day.

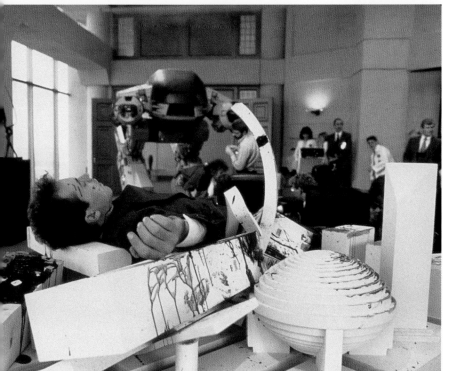

ABOVE
Still from 'RoboCop' (1987)
Bob Morton (Miguel Ferrer) is the ambitious yuppie who jumps upon Dick Jones' failure to deliver the ED-209 and fast tracks the RoboCop program. The success of RoboCop means he will go up the corporate ladder.

RIGHT
On the set of 'RoboCop' (1987)
Paul Verhoeven helps Peter Weller don the RoboCop helmet. Nancy Allen plays Officer Anne Lewis, Murphy's partner and the first to recognise that RoboCop is her former partner.

"Working with Paul Verhoeven, you feel it's not just a movie that you are making, you feel that this guy has a vision and it is going to happen his way or else he is going to die."

Peter Weller

ABOVE
Still from 'RoboCop' (1987)
By removing the helmet, Murphy reasserts his humanity, although there is very little remaining of his physical being. The metal body is now a receptacle for the thoughts and memories of Officer Alex J. Murphy.

LEFT
On the set of 'RoboCop' (1987)
The final showdown with Clarence Boddicker (Kurtwood Smith), the man who killed Murphy.

"He's demanding… but he's only demanding what he should be getting."

Kurtwood Smith

indelibly awful. As Verhoeven has said, "I believe that one guy who was killed in an awful way, like Murphy, is much less dangerous [in terms of inspiring imitators] than having a lot of pictures where you see people working with laser beams, and every second there's a guy on the ground, or there are 40, 50, 60 people killed."[49]

The violence in *RoboCop* is complex and it can elicit contrary responses. When the criminals shoot off Murphy's legs and one arm, and then the corporate bosses order his other arm to be cut off so that they can turn him into RoboCop and make a profit on his fully prostheticized body, the film shows that the corporation is as vicious as the criminals: both are castrating butchers. One response to this traumatic attack would be to recognize the human body's vulnerability and promote a society of law in which everyone will be able to avoid violence. Another response is to arm and armour oneself and to go seeking revenge in the name of justice, like Charles Bronson in *Death Wish* (1974) or Clint Eastwood as *Dirty Harry* (1971). When Murphy adopts the big gun and invincible armour of RoboCop and blows away the bad guys, his vigilante violence provokes cheers from the audience. When RoboCop throws the thuggish Clarence through a series of windows while reading him his rights, we are thrilled to see this criminal broken after what he did to Murphy, and we're glad that laws do not get in the way of retribution.

But even in these vengeful scenes of poetic justice, Verhoeven presents violence in a way that makes us think. When a would-be rapist holds a woman hostage in front of him and when RoboCop shoots the man in the groin between the woman's legs, we may rejoice that the man got what he deserved, but what if RoboCop had hit the woman there? How different would he have been from the rapist? If Murphy was crucified when his body was pierced by the criminals' bullets and if he was then resurrected as RoboCop, we must question what kind of Christ he has become. In the film's climax, RoboCop is filmed as if he were walking on water toward Clarence, the man who had 'crucified' him. As a Christ figure, RoboCop should forgive and save, and as a policeman, he should arrest, but instead RoboCop moves to avenge and assassinate Clarence. As Verhoeven comments, noting the US penchant for preaching religion while acting in decidedly unchristian ways, "RoboCop is a Jesus figure – an American Jesus. Entirely in tune with current ideas here, he says, 'I don't arrest you any more.' He has done with Clarence, the time of turning the other cheek is over. Americans want to be humane, but if they think it takes too long, Christian morality is pushed aside for the moment and they go for their weapons – just like RoboCop."[50]

ABOVE
On the set of 'RoboCop' (1987)
For his first American film, Verhoeven handled a $13 million budget for a 13-week shoot in Dallas. Worldwide, it made $120 million.

OPPOSITE
Still from 'RoboCop' (1987)
Verhoeven's description of RoboCop as the American Jesus is made clear in this shot, where he appears to be walking on the water.

Stills from 'Total Recall' (1990)
Douglas Quaid (Arnold Schwarzenegger) is a
construction worker (top right) with a loving wife
Lori (Sharon Stone, above), who is obsessed
with Mars. He visits Rekall Incorporated (right)
who give memory implants so that Quaid can
take an imaginary holiday to Mars, picking the
secret agent option. However, something goes
wrong and he finds that instead of implanting
new information, Rekall have revealed his old
identity as a secret agent. He is on the run
(opposite top left), is forced to kill the bad guys
(opposite bottom) and removes the bug from his
skull (opposite top right).

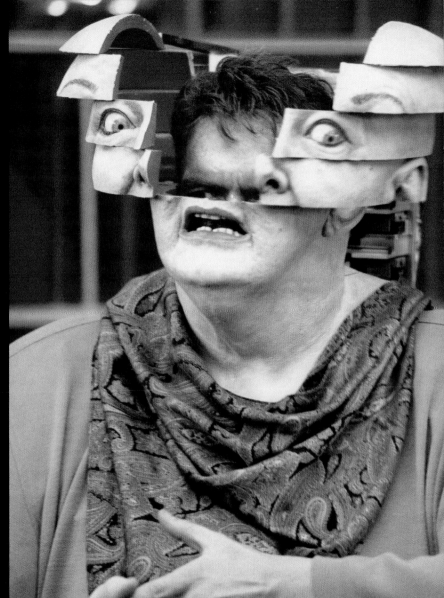

Stills from 'Total Recall' (1990)
Quaid manages to get to Mars disguised as a
woman (right) and after many adventures makes
contact with the leader of the Freedom Brigade,
Kuato (growing out of Marshall Bell, above), who
is trying to save Mars from the dictatorship of
Vilos Cohaagen.

After seeing the success of *RoboCop*, Arnold Schwarzenegger personally requested
that Verhoeven be hired as director of *Total Recall* (1990). Based on the short story
'We Can Remember It for You Wholesale' by famed science-fiction writer Philip K.
Dick, *Total Recall* had been in pre-production hell for almost 20 years. At one point,
David Cronenberg was going to direct it, with Richard Dreyfuss as the star. Then
Bruce Beresford was set to helm the picture, with Patrick Swayze in the lead role. In
the original versions of the script, the hero was a meek accountant, but when
Schwarzenegger took on the part, his bodybuilder's physique required a change in
the role to that of a construction worker. The character's name was also changed
from Quail – which implied timidity and which might have had problematic
associations with Dan Quayle, then Vice President of the United States – to Quaid, a
more manly and muscular name. Indeed, in a movie filled with state-of-the-art
special effects, Schwarzenegger himself may be the biggest special effect of them all:
'In its massive imperishability, the Schwarzenegger body survives whole and sound

despite being punched, mauled, crunched, stabbed, shot, thrown, or kicked in every key scene. These physical blows include punches and kicks to the crotch, with the double implication that the masculinity of this body is as indestructible as its triceps or biceps.'[51] The film was also an opportunity for Schwarzenegger to expand his range as an actor, playing a part that requires him to be naïve and vulnerable at times, and speaking more lines in this one film than he had in all his previous movies put together. Schwarzenegger has given Verhoeven the credit for the improvements in his performance, and Verhoeven in turn has praised Schwarzenegger for how well he took direction: "You can tell Arnold anything about acting or about his hair, the colour of his jacket, or whatever – he will never take it personally. And if he's not good, if he makes a mistake or mispronounces something, then he will change it. ...With many actors, you have to be very careful. A lot of them, if you criticize them [they] will lose confidence or start being nervous. But Arnold is so self-confident. He doesn't have an ego."[52]

ABOVE
Still from 'Total Recall' (1990)
During this adventure Dr. Edgemar (Roy Brocksmith) of Rekall visits Quaid and tells him that none of this is real, that not all of the 'holiday' was implanted, and that Quaid is experiencing a free-form delusion. He must take the red pill to return to reality, otherwise he will lose his mind. Quaid thinks that this is just Cohaagen's ruse to stop him from saving Mars, so he shoots Dr. Edgemar.

PAGES 112/113
Stills from 'Total Recall' (1990)
It seems that Quaid cannot trust anybody. When he comes under attack in his apartment, he discovers that it is his wife Lori, who is an agent working for Cohaagen.

ABOVE
Still from 'Total Recall' (1990)
On Mars, Quaid links up with former lover Melina (Rachel Ticotin, walking on right), a resistance fighter who poses as a prostitute, who has connections to Kuato. She is also exactly like the girl in his dreams, and the girl he selected to be his imaginary girlfriend at Rekall.

RIGHT
Still from 'Total Recall' (1990)
Venusville, the entertainment quarter for the miners, was modelled on Amsterdam's red light district. Here cab driver Benny (Mel Johnson Jr.) samples Tiffany's (Alexia Robinson) wares. The miners mutated because Cohaagen installed cheap domes that did not stop the radiation from getting through. Angry with Cohaagen's oppression, they have formed a resistance movement under Kuato's leadership.

PAGE 117 TOP
Concept painting for 'Total Recall' (1990)
A conceptual drawing of the pyramid mine.

PAGE 117 BOTTOM
Still from 'Total Recall' (1990)
Quaid and Melina in the opening dream sequence

ABOVE
Still from 'Total Recall' (1990)
Melina and Quaid on the run from Helm
(Michael Champion), one of Cohaagen's
henchmen. He does not shoot because he might
shatter the dome.

LEFT
On the set of 'Total Recall' (1990)
Cohaagen uses Quaid to find and kill Kuato, thus
killing off the resistance. However, it turns out
that Quaid is really secret agent Hauser,
Cohaagen's best friend, who volunteered to help.
Now Quaid's mind must be wiped so that
Hauser can return. Here, Verhoeven makes eye
contact with Schwarzenegger while Ronny Cox
(who plays Cohaagen) looks on.

PAGE 116 TOP
Concept painting for 'Total Recall' (1990)
A conceptual drawing of the Mars landscape in
Quaid's dream that opens the film.

PAGE 116 BOTTOM
Still from 'Total Recall' (1990)
This was the last big special effects film to be
made before computer-generated digital images
took over, so a large-scale model was
constructed of the Mars landscape.

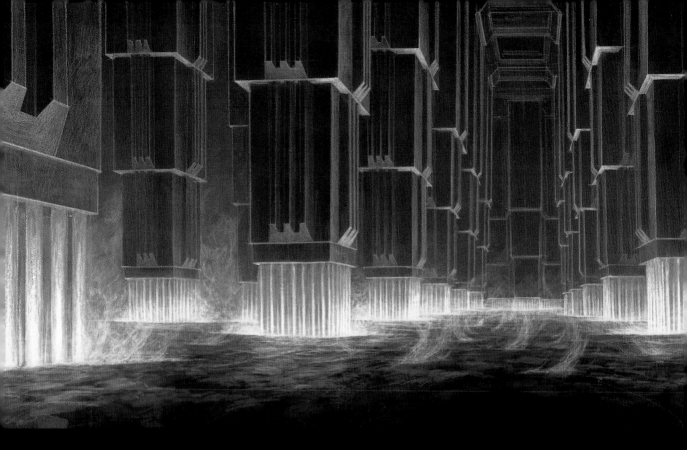

Concept painting for 'Total Recall' (1990)
A conceptual drawing of the alien reactor inside
the pyramid mine. The rods are inserted into the
glacier and air is being generated. There were
45 versions of the script over the many years of
development. Although everybody liked the first
two acts, it took a long time to find a suitable
denouement.

Total Recall was the most expensive movie Verhoeven had ever made up to that
point. While the film was originally budgeted at $48 million (already more than the
combined cost of all Verhoeven's Dutch movies plus *RoboCop*), *Total Recall*'s
complex battle scenes and special effects eventually led to $5 million in cost
overruns, and it was Schwarzenegger who convinced the studio not to cut expensive
scenes from the script and to keep faith with Verhoeven's vision of the film. This
faith was rewarded when the movie grossed $120 million at the US box office and
$270 million worldwide. As *Time* magazine's reviewer noted, 'In today's market $60
million can buy you a sloppy-looking sequel like *Rambo III* [1988], which puts
nothing on the screen but bloat. Or, as here, the fat bankroll can allow canny artists
and artisans to put a mammoth teeming fantasy vision on film.'[53] In addition to its
cost in dollars and cents, the film took a human toll as well. As shooting occurred
on several soundstages in Mexico, cast and crew were sprinting to the toilet and
visiting the studio doctor in droves, having been stricken by Montezuma's revenge.
Just about everyone got sick except Schwarzenegger, whose food was flown in from
L.A. each day and prepared for him in his trailer by his own cook. At one point,
Verhoeven was so dehydrated from vomiting and diarrhoea that he had to be put on
a drip and to direct a scene from an ambulance stretcher, vowing that "Unless I am
dying, we are not gonna stop shooting."[54]

Among those who laboured hardest on the film were its special-effects designers
and technicians. Filmed just before digital compositing would make the creation of
visual effects so much easier, *Total Recall* was one of the last analogue FX
extravaganzas, consisting of objects actually present in front of the camera. Visual
effects supervisor Eric Brevig and his team at Dream Quest Images used real-time
motion control (computer-synchronized camera movements) to combine shots of

actors filmed in front a blue screen with matte paintings and miniatures of red, cratered landscapes. The result was strikingly realistic scenes of living in a fantasy world, of people actually moving around on Mars. Rob Bottin created such special make-up effects as a mutant woman with three breasts, a man with a deformed twin growing out of his chest, a female head that lifts off in horizontal cross-sections to reveal Schwarzenegger's head underneath, and the wildly distorted faces and bulging eyes of characters suffering from depressurization. For their amazingly successful efforts, Bottin and Brevig were awarded an Oscar for Special Achievement in Visual Effects.

As with *RoboCop*, *Total Recall* was originally rated X for violence until certain shots were reduced in length to make them somewhat less graphic, such as those of a drill boring through a man's stomach, a man's arms being chopped off in an elevator accident, and a man's body being used as a human shield for bullets during a shoot-out on an escalator. With its sizable body count (at 74 deaths, the film averages one killing every one-and-a-half minutes) and its snappy Schwarzenegger one-liners ("Consider this a divorce," he says after shooting his wife in the head), *Total Recall* was accused of making violence fun and funny, of trivializing the subject and desensitizing the public. While there may be some truth to this charge, it should also be noted that the violence in *Total Recall* is not bloodless and 'weightless' as it is in such cartoonish action-adventures as *Star Wars* (1977). Instead, Verhoeven injects some brutal realism into the science-fiction fantasy genre by emphasizing the impact of violence on human flesh: blows to the body resound and carry weight; stabbings and bullets draw blood; characters lose limbs and lives. According to editor Frank J. Urioste, Verhoeven's goal was not to exploit violence as a cheap thrill, but to show it as horrific.

Still from 'Total Recall' (1990)
Quaid is hanging on for his life after the dome is breached. One of the ways that Cohaagen keeps control is to charge the miners for the air, and he punishes Venusville for hiding Kuato by starving them of air. By making the air breathable, Quaid is effectively freeing the miners and saving the planet. If he is not dreaming it all...

Certainly, Verhoeven has said that he would not have wasted two years of his working life on a mere action-adventure that looks fantastic but is empty of meaning. What attracted him to the project were its different layers of meaning, which Verhoeven, with his Ph.D. in mathematics and physics, has likened to the Heisenberg Uncertainty Principle. Just as you cannot measure both the position and velocity of a sub-atomic particle at the same time, so the events of *Total Recall* are equivocal, making them hard to follow or pin down. Doug Quaid (Schwarzenegger) may be a hero or a villain. Mars has been colonized by a greedy corporation, which forces people to mine turbinium ore which is used to make military weapons for further conquests. Big business controls the supply of air on Mars (compare the privatization of public services under US Presidents Reagan and Bush), and the people must labour in the mines or they will be put to death by asphyxiation. Already, because the corporation built a cheap dome, the people have been turned into mutants by solar radiation (compare the greenhouse effect which threatens us all). At one point in the film, it seems as though Quaid will be a hero in the people's rebellion, leading the workers in their fight against corporate exploitation. However, at another point it appears that Quaid is instead a villainous double agent, pretending to be on the people's side but actually planted by the corporation to infiltrate and neutralize the workers' resistance. (This ambiguity took on unexpected relevance when, in a 2003 recall election, Schwarzenegger was elected Governor of California. Whether he is, as he claimed, a man of the people, or instead, as some feared, an agent of big business was a matter of heated dispute during the election.)

Related to the hero/villain ambiguity, there is doubt about whether Quaid really saves the people of Mars in the end, starting the alien reactor that brings free air to all, or whether he is actually only dreaming the whole thing, having a virtual vacation or 'ego trip' implanted in his brain by a corporation called Rekall Inc. At one point in the film, a doctor from Rekall tries to convince Quaid that he is not a saviour of the people, but a man having an engineered fantasy. Quaid doesn't know what to believe, but when he sees a bead of sweat roll down the doctor's forehead, he takes this show of fear on the doctor's part as a sign that the man is real and was sent by the corporation to stop Quaid from leading the rebellion. However, it is equally possible that Quaid has merely imagined the sweat on the doctor's brow because Quaid is looking for a reason to believe that he is really a heroic leader on Mars and not just a lowly construction worker having a dream back on Earth.

Similarly, after Quaid has supposedly saved the workers and is about to embrace the woman of his dreams in an ending that seems too good to be true, he wavers: "I just had a terrible thought: what if this *is* a dream?" The woman's reply – "Well, then kiss me quick before you wake up" – hardly solidifies our sense of reality, and the screen's fade to white (instead of the more conventional fade to black) is either the brightest of Hollywood happy endings or, as Verhoeven has suggested it might be, a sign that Quaid's dream has ended with his being lobotomized. Is it still possible to lead a heroic resistance against corporate power, or is any idea of such a rebellion merely an escapist fantasy, no more real than a science-fiction film like *Total Recall* which gives us a triumphant hero we can identify with but never be?

ABOVE
On the set of 'Total Recall' (1990)
Rachel Ticotin and Arnold Schwarzenegger had to perform a large number of scenes in front of blue screens so that the Mars landscape could be added later.

OPPOSITE TOP
On the set of 'Total Recall' (1990)
There is no air on Mars, so Quaid and Melina begin to explode because of the difference in pressure. Rob Bottin created torsos to show the distortion of the faces.

OPPOSITE BOTTOM
On the set of 'Total Recall' (1990)
Many people were needed to operate the torsos. You can see the wires on the floor that lead to the puppets. The operators watch a monitor (the man with the red T-shirt is in front of it) so that they can make the eyes bulge out of their sockets and their tongues protrude.

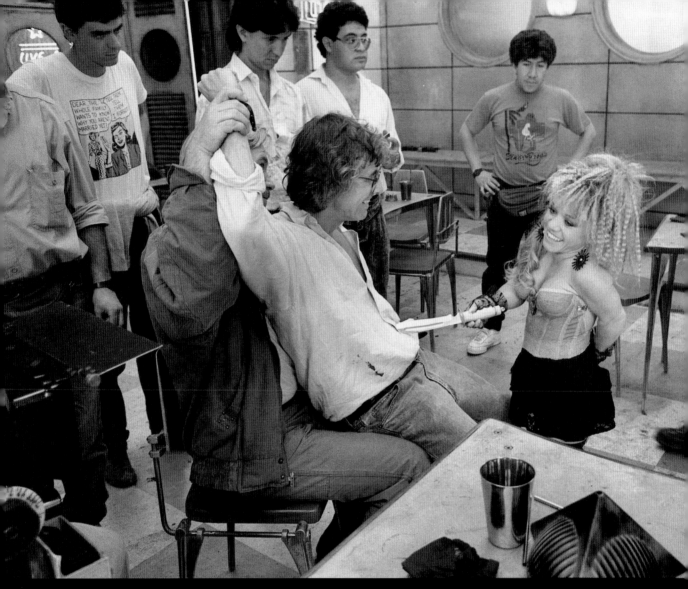

ABOVE
On the set of 'Total Recall' (1990)
Debbie Lee Carrington (as Thumbelina, right)
rehearses the knifing of Helm. Paul Verhoeven
shows how Helm is to be held.

RIGHT
On the set of 'Total Recall' (1990)
Paul Verhoeven shows Rachel Ticotin how to
greet Arnold Schwarzenegger.

ABOVE
On the set of 'Total Recall' (1990)
Verhoeven shows the actors and crew how he
wants a fall to be performed. On the set,
Verhoeven is intent, single-minded and totally
committed. He never asks anybody to do
anything that he would not do himself. For
example, on 'Starship Troopers' a nude shower
scene was required, so Verhoeven and
cinematographer Jost Vacano stripped as well.

LEFT
On the set of 'Total Recall' (1990)
Verhoeven is totally involved in the scene where
the air is being sucked out of the alien reactor.
Ronny Cox is on the floor. Budgeted at $48
million, and one of the most expensive movies at
that time, 'Total Recall' eventually raked in $270
million worldwide.

ABOVE
Still from 'Basic Instinct' (1992)
After Johnny Boz is killed with an ice pick whilst making love, Detective Nick Curran (Michael Douglas) visits Catherine Tramell (Sharon Stone) to question her. It later transpires that the killing was exactly as described in one of Catherine's novels.

OPPOSITE
On the set of 'Basic Instinct' (1992)
The San Francisco setting, the romantic music and the spiralling camera movements, as well as the uncertainty about the blonde woman at the centre of events, all evoke Alfred Hitchcock's 'Vertigo' (1958), a film that Verhoeven has studied many times.

After the large casts and complicated special effects of *RoboCop* and *Total Recall*, it was with some relief that Verhoeven turned to his next venture, *Basic Instinct* (1992), a film on a smaller scale and one that would allow the director, who had by now become more familiar with America, to orchestrate some intimate dialogue and sex scenes between English-speaking actors. Verhoeven had always wanted to make a Hitchcockian thriller, and this seemed like the perfect opportunity. The coolly seductive Catherine Tramell (Sharon Stone) is in the tradition of Hitchcock's icy blondes, provocatively unapproachable and fatally alluring. When detective Nick Curran (Michael Douglas) drives in pursuit of Catherine's car along the twists and turns of a mountain above the sea, we are reminded of Cary Grant and Grace Kelly's serpentine drive along a Monaco hillside in *To Catch a Thief* (1955), and of Jimmy Stewart's tailing Kim Novak around the hilly landscape of San Francisco in *Vertigo*. The erotic banter between Nick and Catherine recalls the sexual innuendo and double entendres of Cary Grant and Eva Marie Saint in *North by Northwest* (1959). To those who would argue that Verhoeven is no Hitchcock in terms of suggestiveness or subtlety, Verhoeven has said that "*Basic Instinct* is a Hitchcock for the nineties, because it's the kind of thing that Hitchcock would perhaps have done if he had been 30 years younger. There are scripts published that Hitchcock did not shoot at the end of his life, and if you see the sexual outrageousness of some of the scenes that he wanted to do and dismissed because he would not have got them through the ratings... [such as the scene of] a girl sitting in the foreground with her lover while her husband is coming up in a boat behind her, and she is masturbating for the guy in the foreground. That was a scene that he wanted to do which would basically be perfect for *Basic Instinct 2*."[55] The graphic sex and violence in *Basic Instinct* are perhaps closest to those in *Frenzy* (Hitchcock's only R-rated film, 1972), and Verhoeven's elevator stabbing scene owes as much to a similar scene in *Dressed to Kill* (1980) by Hitchcock disciple Brian De Palma as it does to the shower stabbing in Hitchcock's *Psycho* (1960). Perhaps the most pervasive Hitchcockian influence on *Basic Instinct* is the musical score, which Verhoeven had Jerry Goldsmith write in the style of Hitchcock's favourite composer, Bernard Herrmann. Ambiguously haunting and threatening, the music is designed to be both erotic and evil at the same time, like romance through a dark mirror.

Originally considered for the role of Nick were Mel Gibson, Kevin Costner and Richard Gere. In the end, the part was given to Michael Douglas, who had already played a man similarly tempted and threatened by the sexual dark side (Glenn Close) in *Fatal Attraction* (1987), and who would soon do so again in *Disclosure* (1994) with Demi Moore. Douglas' stunt-driving abilities also came in handy for the car chase scene in which Nick cuts in and out of oncoming traffic while driving along a mountainside with no guard rails and a 500-foot drop to the sea. During his dialogue scenes, Douglas was so professional as an actor, needing so few takes, that Verhoeven rarely felt the need to speak to him. A rumour grew that Douglas had grown so angry at the lack of directorial compliments that he punched Verhoeven in the nose, but it was later revealed that the director's nosebleed was due to tension and not to an attack from his star.

The studio had originally wanted some actress with an established reputation for the role of Catherine, but the stars who were approached – including Geena Davis, Michele Pfeiffer, Lena Olin, Ellen Barkin, Melanie Griffith, Emma Thompson, Greta Scacchi, Kim Basinger and Julia Roberts – turned down the part, generally because they did not want to be seen totally nude. Verhoeven took a big risk in casting the

Still from 'Basic Instinct' (1992)
Catherine makes friends with interesting people so that she can understand their psychology and study them for her books. She is friendly with Hazel Dobkins (Dorothy Malone, centre), a normal housewife who woke up one day and killed her husband and children for no reason whatsoever.

"Once an actress agrees to take a role that involves nudity, the Screen Actors Guild requires that the producers have her sign a nudity waiver as part of her contract. These negotiations are very specific: what body parts will be visible, if there will be nipples or pubic hair visible, if there will be touching or kissing of the nipples. I schedule these scenes for about six weeks into the production schedule, so the actress can begin to trust me and her co-stars. But you don't want it to be too near the end either, or it's hanging over your head like an operation."

Paul Verhoeven

relatively unknown Sharon Stone, who had impressed him with her performance as Schwarzenegger's duplicitous wife in *Total Recall*. On her first day of shooting, Stone lost confidence, slipping in and out of character, and Verhoeven had to halt filming in order to convince her that she could play the difficult part of a woman who is both charming and diabolical. The next day, as if by magic, Stone had been transformed into the lethally seductive character that would make her famous. In the film's opening scene where a faceless blonde straddles a man during sex and then stabs him to death with an ice pick, no stand-in or body double was used. It is Stone herself playing the part, having toned up her abdominal muscles for the athletic sex and having overcome her nausea at the spouting (fake) blood. Verhoeven has praised Stone highly for her extremely audacious performance in these graphic scenes: "I could not have worked in this way with a known actress; it was because she had nothing to lose that I was able to push her to give so much of herself."[56]

Ironically, given how much she was willing to reveal, Stone has claimed that Verhoeven tricked her into baring her genitals in the now-notorious scene where Catherine uncrosses her legs and flashes her male interrogators. Stone has said that the director asked her to remove her white underwear only because they were causing a distracting reflection, and that he never told her he was going to use a shot of her private parts in the film. But Verhoeven maintains that the leg-uncrossing scene was, like the sex scenes, filmed at the end of the day with only a minimal crew in attendance, and that afterward Stone watched and approved the scene on a video monitor. Whatever the truth regarding this infamously revealing shot, it is certainly the case that Verhoeven storyboarded the sex scenes themselves with great precision, choreographing every angle and movement as in a fight scene: "In most Hollywood movies today, you know, if they fuck it's only done to show that they're fucking, isn't it? They put themselves on top of each other, and all the movement starts, and a lot of dissolves – dissolve to the knees, dissolve to this, dissolve to that – and then that's it. Ahhhh! (*gasps*). And they fall down, and that's the scene. A sex scene needs something more than that. Otherwise, why show it? It's like walking: You don't show people walking if they aren't going somewhere."[57] As Verhoeven points out, the sex scene where Nick and Catherine struggle over who's on top and who will 'die' at the moment of climax is also potentially "a murder scene at the same time. ... [It] has two aspects. There's the sex, but also the question 'Is she going to kill him or not?' Which saves it, of course, from being only a straight love scene."[58]

In *Basic Instinct*, Verhoeven brought a European sexual explicitness to a Hollywood film, and the MPAA was not pleased. The film had to be submitted nine times before it could be granted the R rating which Verhoeven was contractually obligated to obtain and which was deemed necessary for commercial success in America (theatres in suburban malls and video chains like Blockbuster would not carry X or NC-17 rated films). To receive MPAA approval, forty-two seconds of film footage were not so much cut back as replaced with alternate shots that were less graphic in their sex and violence. These included shots of breasts bobbing and bodies grinding during intercourse; Nick's oral sex on Catherine and his taking of Beth from behind; and the bloody bed and elevator stabbings. One thing that did not have to be trimmed from the film was any shot of Douglas' penis, for a clause in the actor's contract had prohibited his member from ever being shown. Unlike in previous films where Verhoeven had mostly treated each sex equally in terms of self-exposure, there was thus a gender imbalance in *Basic Instinct* where Douglas was

Still from 'Basic Instinct' (1992)
Nick shot two tourists whilst on duty (earning him the nickname "Shooter") and was investigated by Lt. Marty Nilsen of internal affairs. At the time he was drinking and doing drugs, but he is clean now, and being counselled by Dr. Beth Garner. However, when Nick finds out that Nilsen sold his confidential file to Catherine, he confronts Nilsen and has to be restrained.

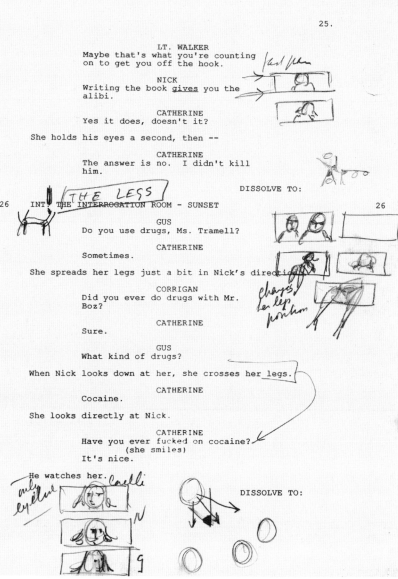

The Interrogation

The film has become famous because of the interrogation scene where Catherine Tramell crosses her legs to reveal her sex to the interrogating officers. She knows that she is naked and so does this as a way of empowering herself and putting the men ill at ease. She is still, unruffled and cool throughout the scene, whereas the men are constantly moving around the room, sweating, getting drinks, taking off their jackets, unbuttoning their shirts and so on. She is unbreakable and impenetrable.

The scene begins with Catherine smoking (opposite). When she is told this is a non-smoking building, she retorts: "What are you going to do? Arrest me for smoking?"

Immediately, we know that she is a powerful woman and that these little people are nothing to her.

The staging and framing of the interrogation is also important. Catherine is framed either as a full figure in bright lights, or as a figure higher than the group of police officers, giving her more presence and power in the relationship. She is lit brightly and the police are in shadows. So she is big and important and the police are little and unimportant.

As can be seen from Paul Verhoeven's personal copy of the script, Joe Eszterhas' dialogue remains unchanged in the final edit of the film,

but Verhoeven changes the point where Catherine's legs are crossed. Instead of crossing her legs in reaction to Gus' question (which could be interpreted as a defensive gesture), she reveals her sex when she asks Nick if he had ever fucked on cocaine. This completely changes the balance of power in the room and puts her in control. Not only is she asking Nick if he would like to fuck her, but she is revealing that she knows something about Nick's past. We now know that Catherine is interested in Nick and that she is going after him, either for sex, for research for a book, to kill him for pleasure, or for all of these reasons.

naked but not exposed while Stone bared all. Nevertheless, Verhoeven did even things out somewhat by showing Douglas' vulnerable bare buttocks and back, and by revealing the flaccid organ of the first male murder victim.

If *Basic Instinct* raised the conservative hackles of the MPAA, it also incited the ire of political groups on the left. Gay activists disrupted filming on San Francisco locations by throwing paint bombs, blowing whistles and getting people in passing cars to honk their horns (signs tricked drivers into honking to show their support for American troops in the Gulf War and for the local 49ers football team). Verhoeven and the studio took the position that "Censorship by street action will not be tolerated"[59] and they obtained a restraining order against the activists, barring them from venturing within one hundred yards of location filming, but some protesters defied this injunction and were placed under arrest for disturbing the shoot. When Verhoeven and writer Joe Eszterhas agreed to meet with representatives from GLAAD (the Gay and Lesbian Alliance Against Defamation) and other activist groups, the protesters demanded that the film be rescripted and recast to make it less homophobic and misogynistic, or they would not allow the movie to be made in San Francisco. Douglas' leading role as Nick should be changed to that of a lesbian detective played by Kathleen Turner in order to show that a homosexual could be the hero. Either the killer should be changed to a man, or the bisexual Catherine and her lesbian friend Roxy should murder women as well as men so that bisexuals and lesbians would not be viewed as man-haters.

Eszterhas, who had earlier walked off the picture for a brief time because he feared that Verhoeven's explicit approach to the film's sex scenes threatened to make the movie pornographic, sided with the protesters, saying that his eyes had been opened to the insensitivity and stereotyping in his own screenplay. Though he did not accede to the drastic changes proposed by the activists, which would have cost millions of dollars in recasting and reshooting, Eszterhas did make some alterations in the script: now Nick would first ask Beth's permission before having rough sex; Nick would comment that "A lot of the best people I've met in this town are gay"[60]; and a disclaimer would be included at the start of the film that 'The movie you are about to see is fiction.'[61] When Verhoeven rejected Eszterhas' changes, a strange situation developed in which a director was defending the integrity of a script against its own author (who had been paid a record $3.3 million for it). Eszterhas publicly disowned and denounced his original script, but later stated after seeing the completed picture that Verhoeven had been right not to weaken the characters by making changes.

When the film was released, activists picketed theatres in an effort to persuade moviegoers not to attend. The protesters carried signs saying 'Kiss My Ice Pick', 'Hollywood Promotes Anti-Gay Violence' and 'Catherine Did It!' – this last sign an attempt to spoil the ending of the movie. Throughout the controversy, Verhoeven defended the protesters' right to free speech, but he criticized their disruptive tactics: "Fascism is not in raising your voice, the fascism is in not accepting the no."[62] In the end, the activists probably succeeded in raising public consciousness about homophobia, but they did not manage to prevent the film from being made or seen. Instead, all the publicity actually helped to make *Basic Instinct* a tremendous *succès de scandale*. Budgeted at $49 million, the film grossed $118 million in the US and $353 million worldwide.

Some reviewers were repelled by *Basic Instinct*'s combination of sex and violence: 'Call me a prude, but it's not sexy watching an erotic thriller in which every time a

ABOVE
Still from 'Basic Instinct' (1992)
After Nilsen is shot dead, Nick is suspended from duty pending an investigation because of his earlier argument with Nilsen. Nick relaxes by going out with Catherine. He meets her at a church-like disco, where Catherine is dancing provocatively with Roxy (Leilani Sarelle), her butch lesbian lover.

OPPOSITE
Still from 'Basic Instinct' (1992)
Catherine goes with Nick, much to Roxy's disgust, and they make love. Nick calls it "the fuck of the century". Catherine thinks it is good for a start.

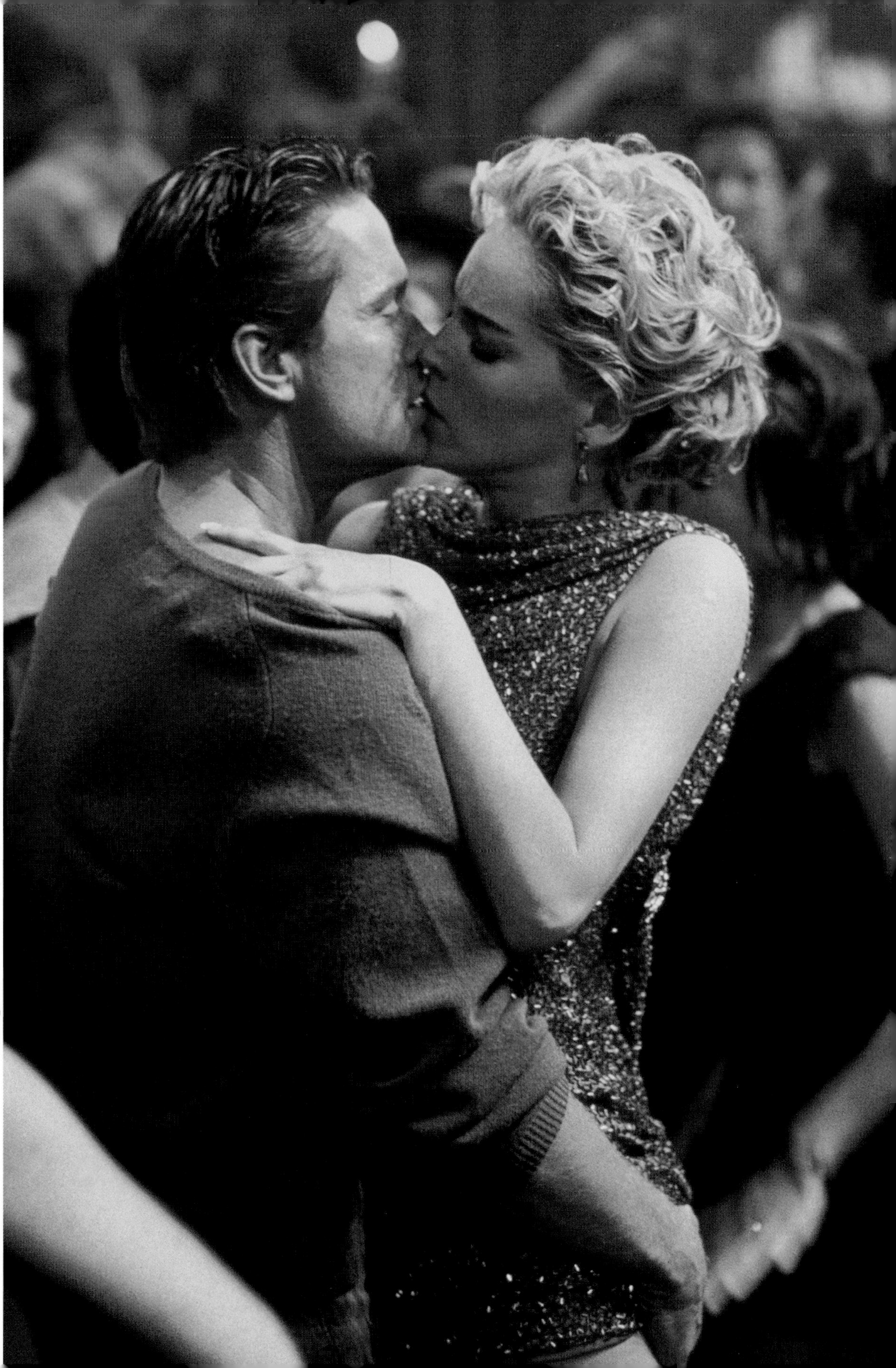

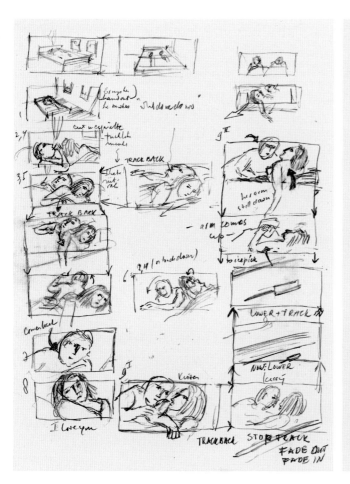

152   INT. HIS BEDROOM - LATER   152

The Stones play "Sympathy for the Devil" in the b.g.; the
MUSIC is low.

They lie next to each other on the bed. The CAMERA faces
them. He lies, staring at the ceiling, on the left side
of the bed, smoking a cigarette. She is curled away from
him toward the right side of the bed. A long beat, then --

                    CATHERINE
          What do we do now, Nick?

                    NICK
              (after a long beat)
          We fuck like minks. We raise
          rugrats. We live happily ever
          after.

We see her right arm go to the side of the bed and
over. He stares at the ceiling.

                    CATHERINE
          I hate rugrats.

                    NICK
              (after a long beat)
          We fuck like minks. We forget
          the rugrats. We live happily ever
          after.

We see from an ANGLE to the right of the bed now.

Her face is expressionless. Her right arm dangles over
the right side of the bed. Her right hand is clenched.
Is she holding something in it against her arm?

We see them from an ANGLE to the left side of the bed.

He turns his body away from her to put out his cigarette.

We see her behind him slowly turning towards him and the
CAMERA. A beat, and he turns towards her.

They look at each other. A long beat as the SONG gets
louder. We see them in CLOSEUP. We don't see her right
arm.

                    CATHERINE
              (in a whisper)
          I love you.

A beat, and he kisses her. The CAMERA BACKS AWAY from them
slowly to the right side of the bedroom as they kiss, and
we --

                    FADE TO BLACK.

                                                    111A

                    CATHERINE
          One last thing, Nick...
              (a beat)
          I love you.

Her face tenses as she starts to pull the trigger, then
they both move with a shudder.

Her expression changes. She stares at him strangely. She
looks down.

An icepick is sticking in her heart. Nick's hand grips
the handle.

                    NICK
          I love you too.

Her eyes go glassy. The gun drops from her hand. Her body
goes limp.

She hangs in his arms, dead. He lets her drop to the
floor.

Nick looks down at her.

Her body rests on his feet. His feet pull out from under
her dead weight. The feet walk out of frame.

Catherine lies there -- in a growing puddle of blood.

                    THE END

These script pages (above) show the final scene between Nick and Catherine. Verhoeven's detailed thumbnails show the positions and movements of the characters and camera so that information is revealed and withheld.

Although Verhoeven eventually used Eszterhas' first draft of the script, he had actually rewritten it four times with Gary Goldman to find ways to improve it. By doing this, Verhoeven had found the nuts and bolts of the story's construction and eventually realised that the first draft was the best draft. However, this process was important for Verhoeven because it was only by destroying the script that he could understand it fully. He goes through the same process on each movie.

Alternative endings were written, as can be seen from script page 111A (left) and Verhoeven's thumbnails on the right of page 109 (above), but in these either Nick killed Catherine or Catherine killed Nick, neither of which are satisfactory. The ending as filmed has Nick and Catherine live together, with Catherine revealed as the killer. Since, in Verhoeven's eyes, Catherine is the Devil, this means that Nick has been tempted back to the dark side of his personality.

couple does it, one of them gets it with an ice pick'[63]; 'The sex resembles a violent contact sport, with a scoring system known only to the players'[64]; 'It makes you feel dirty in the morning.'[65] However, other critics championed the film for its strong female characters: 'Basic Instinct is undoubtedly exploitative, but it's also unsettling – it's as if the female sex toys in a garden-variety porn flick suddenly developed an unpredictable, shocking, vengeful autonomy'[66]; 'I thought it was a gas to see a woman on the screen in a powerful enough position to let it all hang out and not be punished for it in the end'[67]; 'a dyke with two Ferraris who kills men? Now that's a positive image!'[68]

Whatever the power dynamic between Verhoeven and Stone in filming the leg-uncrossing scene, it's worth noting that in terms of what is going on between the characters in the film, Catherine succeeds in using her sex as a weapon in this scene, turning the lechery of her male interrogators against them, holding these voyeurs captive in her gaze. As Stone has said, "If you have a vagina and a point of view, that's a deadly combination."[69] It's possible to see the femmes fatales in *Basic Instinct* not as motiveless killers or thrill-seeking devils, but as women striking out against male sexual and social domination. Nick seems intent on proving his masculinity by "nailing" Catherine – conquering her in bed and pinning down the mystery of her sex. When Nick and Catherine make love, they struggle over who's on top. In the film's final bedroom scene, Catherine seems about to stab Nick with an ice pick – until he admits that maybe he doesn't need her to have his children ("forget the rug rats"). It is only when Nick stops being a "Shooter" – violently penetrating, imposing his will – that Catherine can embrace him rather than striking back.

Is there homophobia in *Basic Instinct*? Of course there is. When most of the female characters in the film (Catherine, Roxy, Beth) are lesbian/bisexual and are also a proven or potential murderers, one can hardly deny that the film exploits the cliché of the dyke with a dagger (or an ice pick or a gun). However, the film's negative stereotypes are so blatantly over the top that it is nearly impossible to take them seriously, suggesting that the movie is in fact mocking homophobia, ridiculing male fears of sexually desiring and independent women. If "*Basic Instinct* is an Americanization of *The Fourth Man*" as Verhoeven has noted,[70] then perhaps this film is similarly coloured by male fantasies and fears. Catherine is not so much a real woman as a male projection of dread and desire regarding female difference. Her independent sexuality excites sadistic macho fantasies of taking her from her lesbian lovers, capturing her and punishing her for her elusiveness. But that same female sexual power gives rise to fears of castration as well as masochistic fantasies of 'dying' in her arms, of being relieved of the burden of machismo and giving himself over to her.

At the end of a classic film noir, the mystery is solved and the femme fatale is caught and punished – the woman is "nailed". But at the end of *Basic Instinct*, Verhoeven's contemporary film noir, Catherine remains a mystery to the men and empowered to define herself beyond the sexist clichés of good wife or femme fatale.

"For a movie like Basic Instinct*, it would have been very bad to show it to a preview audience. I'm sure all the cards would have come back saying the ending was too ambiguous. The studio would have read these cards and said people are confused. And everybody would have insisted to end it in a conventional way, like he kills her, she kills him, or whatever. But nobody would have dared to do what is there now."*

Paul Verhoeven

ABOVE
On the set of 'Basic Instinct' (1992)
Jan de Bont and Paul Verhoeven discuss a shot. Jan de Bont went on to a successful career as the director of 'Speed' (1994), and 'Lara Croft Tomb Raider: The Cradle of Life' (2003).

OPPOSITE
On the set of 'Basic Instinct' (1992)
The production was fraught with problems. Gay pressure groups got hold of the script and protested that it was anti-gay, going so far as to disrupt the filming. Producer Alan Marshall put a restraining order on the protestors and had to make citizen arrests. There were arguments and reconciliations between Verhoeven and Eszterhas. After Sharon Stone saw the film, she protested about revealing her sex in the interrogation scene, even though she had been fully consulted about it at the time. Perhaps she was protesting because she realised that American audiences would be largely shocked and embarrassed by the scene. In truth, it is one part of a brave and magnificent performance.

After three Hollywood hits in a row – *RoboCop*, *Total Recall* and *Basic Instinct* – Verhoeven finally had the box-office clout to do something really audacious: make a major movie that he would not have to cut to achieve an R rating. Over lunch at the Ivy restaurant in Beverly Hills, the director patched things up with writer Joe Eszterhas, and as the two got to talking about the big MGM musicals they both loved, Verhoeven confessed that he had always wanted to shoot a musical, but not the old-fashioned kind. Eszterhas suggested they make a film set in contemporary Las Vegas, an idea that eventually led to that volcanic combination of stripteases, lap dances, S&M dance numbers and swimming-pool sex we now know as *Showgirls* (1995). On the strength of his previous box-office successes, Verhoeven got pre-approval in his contract with MGM/United Artists to make an NC-17 movie, thus becoming the first director in history to be granted such no-holds-barred freedom by a major Hollywood studio. In return for complete creative control and the right of final cut, Verhoeven agreed to defer 70% of his $6 million director's fee until the time when – or if – the film turned a profit. Verhoeven figured that if the studio was taking such a big gamble, he should be willing to share the risk. And what a gamble it was! Despite the surprising success of 1969's *Midnight Cowboy* (the only X-rated film ever to win an Academy Award for Best Picture), the studios essentially stopped making such films the very next year when both *Myra Breckinridge* (1970) and *Beyond the Valley of the Dolls* (1970) bombed at the box office. Then, in 1990, when a new rating was created to distinguish serious adult films from pornography, the studios tried again with the first NC-17 movie, *Henry & June* (1990), but only one hundred theatres agreed to screen it and it proved to be a financial disaster.

Knowing that a $38 million, NC-17-rated movie like *Showgirls* was a long shot for success, the studio began an aggressive marketing campaign. The interest of theatre audiences was piqued by a summer teaser that described "a movie so erotic... so dangerous... so controversial... that we can't show you a thing", followed later by a trailer playing up the fact that this was another steamy film by the Verhoeven-Eszterhas duo that had brought the world *Basic Instinct*: "Last time they took you to the edge. This time they're taking you all the way." In addition to poster ads of Elizabeth Berkley's revealing cleavage and long bare leg which were displayed on airplanes, taxis, buses, bus stops and on billboards over Times Square and along Sunset Boulevard, there were 250,000 copies of a promotional video trailer with sexy scenes from the movie distributed to video stores for free rental. On a special *Showgirls* website, which initially received more than a million hits a day, visitors could view nude photos and chat with Berkley about the film. Berkley also appeared on David Letterman's late-night talk show to demonstrate the art of lap dancing.

While most of the publicity focused on sexual enticement ('Leave your inhibitions at the door'; 'Beyond your wildest dreams. Beyond your wildest fantasies'; 'Sensual. Controversial. Available'), Eszterhas promoted the film as a morality tale, taking out a full-page ad in *Variety* to argue that 'The movie shows that dancers in Vegas are often victimized, humiliated, used, verbally and physically raped by the men who are at the power centers of that world... [The] advertising people have devised a tag line "Leave your inhibitions at the door" to sell a movie which is about a young woman who leaves her ambitions at the door to save her soul... I implore you not to let... misguided, fast-buck advertising... influence your feelings about *Showgirls*.'[71] In interviews, Eszterhas complained that "It's a chauvinistic position to [advertise *Showgirls*] on the sports pages, because of its

OPPOSITE
Stills from 'Showgirls' (1995)
Nomi Malone (Elizabeth Berkley) hitch-hikes to Las Vegas in search of fame and fortune, but has her bag stolen, so begins her ascent from nothing. She starts pole- and lap-dancing at Cheetah's to make money.

PAGES 138/139
On the set of 'Showgirls' (1995)
Director Paul Verhoeven (left), who was the first director in history to be contractually obligated to deliver an NC-17 film, and writer Joe Eszterhas interviewed over 200 Las Vegas dancers / strippers / producers, etc. about their experiences and incorporated their stories into

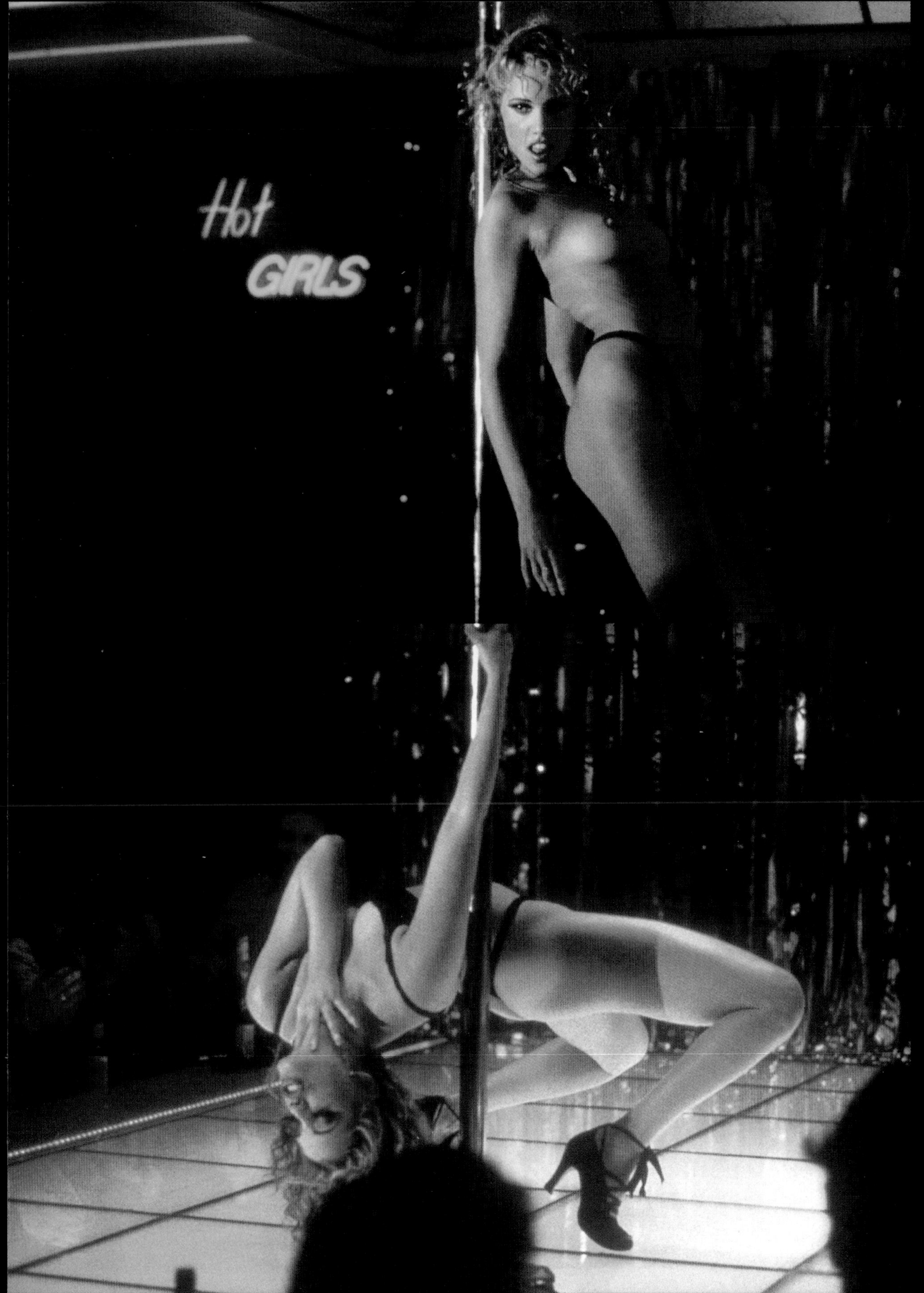
Hot
GIRLS

"women will respond to this movie in the same ways that they responded to *Flashdance*" (also scripted by Eszterhas),[72] and the writer went on to encourage women under 17 to use fake IDs so that they could get in to see his edifying movie. Probably the most innovative approach to marketing the film was Gina Gershon's comment on CNN's *Showbiz Today* that *Showgirls* is "the perfect Bob Dole movie... It's all about morals and values. ...It just happens to be done topless."[73] (Gershon plays Cristal Connors, reigning queen of the Vegas show world and Nomi's rival.) This multifaceted marketing push managed to break through the ban on advertising and screening NC-17 films, raising high hopes for big box-office returns. Ads ran in most major markets, with only some Bible Belt newspapers and one television network (NBC) abstaining. Showings were booked at 1,388 theatres, so *Showgirls* would open almost as wide as *Basic Instinct*, with only two theatre chains based in the American South refusing to screen the movie. The gamble seemed set to pay off.

For Elizabeth Berkley, this film was the gamble of a lifetime. The 21-year-old English literature major had had a part on the TV sitcom *Saved by the Bell* and had just missed out on movie roles that went to Winona Ryder and Uma Thurman instead. *Showgirls* could make Berkley a star, as *Basic Instinct* had done for Sharon Stone. "I knew it was just going to take that one person to say, 'I believe in her and this is who I want,' and that happened with Paul [Verhoeven]," Berkley said.[74] Like the character of Nomi she plays in *Showgirls*, who pushes her way from obscurity to fame as the lead in a Las Vegas revue, Berkley aggressively pursued her part in the film, calling producer Charles Evans before casting had even begun and identifying herself on the phone as "Nomi from *Showgirls*", then later walking into Verhoeven's office and declaring, "There's no one else who can play this role, so you might as well stop looking."[75] Certainly, the link between herself and Nomi as potential future stars was not lost on Berkley and may well have contributed to the startling intensity of her performance. As she has noted, "We were filming the scene where Nomi's about to go into her audition at the Stardust and she's saying, 'I can't do this.' And I suddenly thought, *I* can't. *I* can't do it. I looked up and saw the sign that said CRISTAL CONNORS IS A GODDESS, and for a second I saw ELIZABETH BERKLEY STARRING IN *SHOWGIRLS*, and it was *so emotional*."[76]

To Berkley's misfortune, her hopes of becoming a star did not come true. While Nomi receives rave reviews, Berkley was subjected to some of the most cruelly negative notices ever suffered by an aspiring actress. Critics described her as having 'the non-personality and permanently gaping mouth of an inflatable doll.'[77] Her dances were 'absurd epileptic acts'[78] that had her 'moving as spastically as a rag doll in a hurricane.'[79] Her body parts were deemed better actors than her face: '*Showgirls* requires that Berkley spend at least half her time topless, and it could be argued, in the interest not of prurience but of pure dramatic method, that her breasts are more expressive than her face. Looking closely at her mouth, I saw to my surprise that even her lipstick was wearing lipstick, and the sheer weight of Revlon, or whatever, seems to restrict the free play of her feelings from the neck up.'[80] In sum, the critical consensus on Berkley was that 'She can't act, she overacts, she explodes in every scene, ruining the film.'[81] As a result of these vicious reviews, Berkeley's career was nipped in the bud. Her agent dropped her after *Showgirls*, and she has since been relegated mostly to TV roles.

Verhoeven, too, took a beating from the critics, and *Showgirls* became his first Hollywood flop. Jack Mathews of *Newsday* called it 'the worst movie of 1995', something a high school senior would be embarrassed to submit to *Penthouse*.'[82]

ABOVE
Still from 'Showgirls' (1995)
Nomi is like an animal that has been bred in the wild, with no knowledge of culture but with an instinctive knowledge of what she wants and how to get it. She has the money for a Versace dress, so she buys it, but pronounces the brand as "Ver-sayce". Her best friend is Molly Abrams (Gina Ravera). Throughout the film she acts as Nomi's conscience.

OPPOSITE
Still from 'Showgirls' (1995)
When Nomi gets the opportunity to audition for a proper Las Vegas show, the producers discover that she has that special quality they need: the ability to sell her sex to every member of the audience.

Still from 'Showgirls' (1995)
As Nomi ruthlessly moves up the ranks of dancers, she lusts for the number one spot, currently occupied by Cristal Connors (Gina Gershon, left). This conflict of both admiring a star and jealously wanting to take their position has overtones of 'All About Eve' (1950), which is why people have sometimes referred to 'Showgirls' as 'All About Evil'.

The film critic for *Variety* wrote that 'the only positive thing there is to say about *Showgirls* is that the sensibility of the film perfectly matches that of its milieu. Impossibly vulgar, tawdry and coarse.'[83] And Richard Corliss of *Time* magazine said that *Showgirls*' NC-17 rating should be for its 'Obscene level of incompetence, excessive inanity in the story line, gross negligence of the viewer's intelligence, a prurient interest in the quick buck', and he called the movie 'one of those delirious, hilarious botches that could be taught in film schools as a How Not To.'[84] *Showgirls* had the dishonour of winning a record number of Golden Raspberry Awards, including Worst Music, Worst Original Song ('Walk into the Wind, a.k.a. Love Theme from the Rape Scene'), Worst Actress, Worst New Star, Worst Screenplay,

Still from 'Showgirls' (1995)
For the 'Avenging Angels' number this love/hate relationship is perfectly evoked with the S&M clothing and the embrace/kiss choreography.

Worst Picture and most galling of all, Worst Director. Showing courage and a sense of humour, Verhoeven became the first director in history to attend the Razzies ceremony and personally accept his award for Worst Director. Verhoeven's acceptance speech was quite a crowd-pleaser, but it still revealed the hurt behind the humour: "When I was making movies in the Netherlands my films were judged by the critics as decadent, perverted and sleazy... so I moved to the United States. This was ten years ago. In the meantime, my movies are criticized as being decadent, perverted and sleazy in *this* country... I am very glad that I got all these awards, because it certainly means that I am accepted here and that I am part of this great American society."[85] After outcries in the Netherlands against *Turkish Delight* and

"I was at a press junket last week and when I left the room, some of the participants would pass by and whisper, 'I like Showgirls.' They wouldn't say it in public of course."

Paul Verhoeven

143

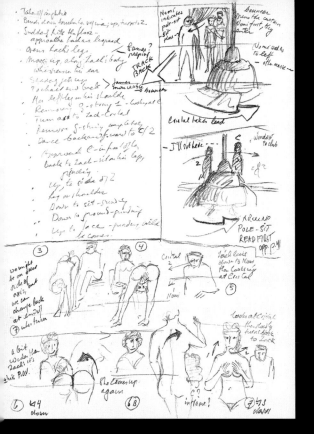
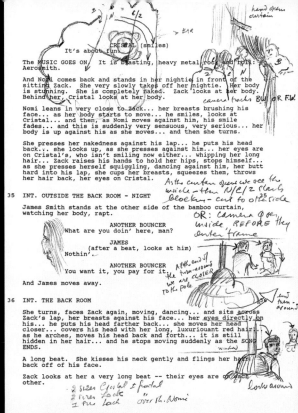

Script pages for 'Showgirls' (1995)

The lap dance scene continues the love/hate relationship between Nomi and Cristal, yet at the same time demonstrates the way everybody manipulates everybody else. Cristal pays $500 to watch Nomi dance for Zack. In reality, Cristal wants Nomi, and her body positions mirror Zack's, as though Cristal is imagining herself in Zack's position. As Nomi dances aggressively on Zack she is looking at Cristal, conveying the message that she wants to fuck Cristal.

'I think that the First Amendment is one of the cornerstones of democracy, a true sign of strength. It tells us that in American society you can say or show whatever you want to say or show – even if it is irritating, disgusting, unpleasant, shocking, or offensive to everyone else.'

Spetters, Verhoeven had left his home country, but now his Hollywood films – *Basic Instinct* and *Showgirls* – were being savaged by the critics. Moreover, unlike *Basic Instinct*, *Showgirls* bombed at the box office. The $38 million movie recouped only about half its cost from US theatres. Verhoeven was shaken by the failure, as he admitted in interviews: "It makes you lose your confidence... You question yourself in any way: 'Am I too old? Am I out of touch? Am I too personal or is my personality so perverted that the audience rejects it?'"[86]

What went wrong with *Showgirls*? It's always possible that Verhoeven simply gave puritan America more sex than it could handle in a mainstream film. People may just have been too ashamed to attend – to be seen in public as the kind of person who would go to such a movie. Evidence for this lies in the excellent revenues generated by home-movie rentals of *Showgirls* which, when combined with strong theatre attendance by less inhibited European audiences, eventually helped the film to turn a profit. Another explanation for the film's box-office failure might be that it was trying to do two contradictory things. Verhoeven basically says as much when he describes *Showgirls* as having "a layer of brutal realism on the one hand and a layer of fairytale fantasy on the other."[87] Just as we are enjoying the fantasy of Nomi's sexual allure and her rags-to-riches rise to showgirl stardom, the film ruins our pleasure with a brutal exposé of greed and sleaze in the Vegas show world. Is Nomi a goddess or a whore? Is the movie meant to arouse us, or to force us to confront the dark side of our desires? Verhoeven himself seems torn about his intentions. In one interview, he says that "The only

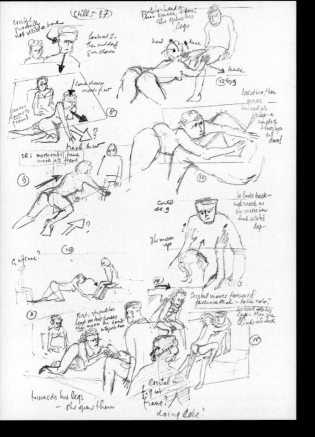

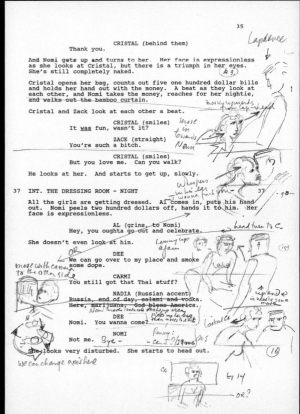

home in a state of excitement and, thinking of the film, make love or masturbate,"[88] while in another interview Verhoeven maintains that "*Showgirls* is not pornographic. It isn't trying to get an erection from you. It's more the contrary. This movie puts sex in such a perspective that it is anti-erotic. Sex is always used as a tool in the movie, as a possibility to get rich or to get a better job."[89] Based on conversations with over two hundred strippers, dancers, and other people in the Vegas entertainment world, *Showgirls* certainly has a muckraking side, and what it reveals about sexual exploitation may have been a little too real for audiences who wanted to get lost in sexual fantasy. Just when Nomi achieves fame as the lead dancer in a Vegas revue which seems designed to excite us, she renounces her stardom, believing that it is merely another form of prostitution, which makes us feel that *we* have been exploiting her.

Ironically, Verhoeven has said that the *least* realistic thing about *Showgirls* is Nomi's discovery of her moral identity – she goes from 'no me' to 'know me' – and her decision to leave Las Vegas and its corrupting fame: "In reality, most people who are willing to compromise everything and finally have the prize in their hands don't throw it away as Nomi does. ...This theme of redemption is part of American mythology. American movies are filled with these fairytales in which everything comes out right and everybody goes to the seashore. It is an illusion that is supported by the whole culture, and is probably part of the larger unwillingness to look at unpleasant realities."[90]

Despite its disastrous debut, *Showgirls* has since gone on to become a cult classic. At special midnight screenings of the movie, audiences shout along with the

Script pages for 'Showgirls' (1995)
Verhoeven's detailed choreography of characters and camera for this scene shows the importance he attached to it. In fact the finished film goes further, with Nomi straddling Zack with her back to him, thrusting her bottom back and forth as she looks at Cristal. This reinforces the point of the scene.

"America was puritan from the start, and I've always had more problems here than in Europe, but it's worse now with this fundamentalist right-wing government. Ashcroft is fundamentalist, Bush is a born-again, and I think they all think that God's on their side. And God doesn't fuck, so we shouldn't either."

Paul Verhoeven

Still from 'Showgirls' (1995)
Irritated by the harsh reviews, Verhoeven joked that: "Part of the audience will go home in a state of excitement and, thinking of the film, make love or masturbate. That's not so bad."

characters' memorably awful lines and lap dance in imitation of Nomi. A favourite on the film festival circuit, *Showgirls* is sometimes 'annotated' by guest speakers, as when David Schmader paid tribute to Berkley's co-star, Gina Gershon: "Gay men have long embraced strong, sassy women who survive hideous adversity with wit and style... For most gay-martyr icons – Judy, Liza, Tina – this adversity stretched over decades. But for Gina Gershon, this beloved-martyr status was earned simply by Gershon surviving the 2 1/2 hours of *Showgirls* with her camp-o-meter on high and her dignity intact – almost."[91] Director John Waters has described *Showgirls* as "funny, stupid, dirty and filled with cinematic clichés; in other words, perfect,"[92] while feminist scholar Linda Williams has said, "I predict that *Showgirls* will

reemerge one day, like Nomi and Cristal from their papier-mâché volcano, in triumphant glory to gain the praise that it deserves."[93] On his end, Verhoeven has been happy to receive even these campy compliments after all the critical attacks on his film: "Maybe this kind of ritualistic cult popularity isn't what I intended," he has said, "but it's like the resurrection after the crucifixion."[94]

Still from 'Showgirls' (1995)
Nomi's ruthlessness reaches the point where she pushes Cristal down the stairs so that she has to go on stage in the lead role. Nomi becomes the new 'Goddess' and she revels in the star treatment that she has craved for so long.

"*I always read the reviews. And of course it's annoying and painful when they trash your movie. But sometimes, and this is even worse,*

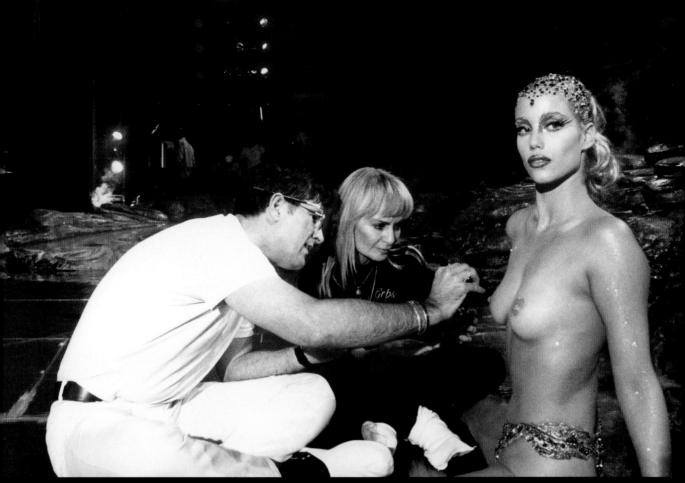

ABOVE
On the set of 'Showgirls' (1995)

LEFT
On the set of 'Showgirls' (1995)
Paul Verhoeven directs Elizabeth Berkley's first
appearance in the 'Goddess' number.

OPPOSITE
On the set of 'Showgirls' (1995)
Nomi simmers with naked ambition. She is a
dark, unlikeable leading character. We watch her
to see how far she is willing to go to get what she
wants. Like Kirk Douglas' boxer in 'Champion'
(1949), she is willing to go all the way.

"Arguably it was the awkward yet provocative
attempt of Showgirls *to say something about*
America – Hollywood in particular – that spelled
its commercial doom: it's a film that
fundamentally said, 'We're all whores, aren't we?'
and the American public answered, in effect,
'Speak for yourself.'"

Jonathan Rosenbaum

"Someone [at Sony Pictures] said to me, 'I think these flags look like Nazi flags,' and I said, 'Well, they're not. The Nazis didn't have green-and-white flags.' But of course they are Nazi flags and the costumes were based on Nazi uniforms."

Paul Verhoeven

Still from 'Starship Troopers' (1997)
The film revolves around three high-school friends in a militaristic future, sports jock Johnny Rico (Casper Van Dien), the beautiful and refined Carmen Ibanez (Denise Richards) and egghead Carl Jenkins (Neil Patrick Harris), who join the military because it is their duty as good citizens.

Verhoeven's next project was a return to the tried-and-true genre of science fiction in which he had had two of his biggest hits, *RoboCop* and *Total Recall*. Based on a 1959 Hugo Award-winning novel by Robert Heinlein, *Starship Troopers* (1997) was, at its most basic level, a story about young adults fighting giant bugs in space. Drawing inspiration from such 1950s films as *Tarantula* (1955), *Them!* (1954) and *The War of the Worlds*, the movie would pit humans against extraterrestrial insects in an all-out war for survival. Of the film's $100 million budget, $40 million would be devoted solely to special effects. Two hundred of the film's six hundred FX shots would contain computer-generated bugs, as compared to fewer than fifty CG dinosaur shots in *Jurassic Park* (1993). One of the first decisions Verhoeven made was that the bugs would be biologically realistic rather than anthropomorphic. The insects in Heinlein's novel stood upright, wore uniforms, and fired weapons, but Verhoeven didn't want shots of a giant cockroach holding a ray gun, or a man in a suit with a funny crab claw. Instead, designer Craig Hayes was asked to make the bugs both convincing as insects and palpably frightening. The bugs would use their own bodies as weapons, and they would be organized in a quasi-military hierarchy, with Warrior Bugs (ground troops) killing with their claws and jaws, Tanker Bugs (tanks) spraying corrosive fire, Plasma Bugs (heavy artillery) ejecting plasma bursts at incoming spaceships, Hopper Bugs (air force) flying and swooping down to attack and a Brain Bug (military intelligence) controlling it all with its hive mind.

To animate the bugs, Verhoeven chose Phil Tippett, who had done such a terrific job on the ED-209 sequences for *RoboCop*. Technology had come a long way since then, and Tippett was now able to use a Digital Input Device that allowed stop-motion animators to move the limbs on scale models of the insects, and to have these movements linked to a computer which converted them directly into the digital environment. The on-screen result was digital bugs that nevertheless moved with realistic weight and mass. The Warrior Bugs were fast and ferocious, while also appearing to weigh over 1500 pounds each. When texture, sheen, and shadowing were digitally added to the bugs, they looked completely photorealistic and lethally lifelike during the battle scenes which occur in broad daylight. Since the bugs weren't added until post-production, the actors were presented with a problem during live-action filming: how to engage in a life-and-death struggle with literally nothing there to fight. To help with this problem, flags on poles were used to ensure correct eye-lines, and Verhoeven himself would be off-camera jumping around and screaming like the bugs so that the actors would have something to react to.

As with the insects, Verhoeven also insisted on a similar realism when it came to the spaceships. For this he turned to Scott Anderson at Sony Imageworks, who had won an Oscar for *Babe* (1995). Unlike the small, sleek fighters in *Star Wars* which zipped around the galaxy, the future spacecraft envisioned by Verhoeven were not streamlined because there is no air or water resistance in space. Anderson designed miniature models that nevertheless appeared on screen to have the heft and bulk of aircraft carriers or oil tankers, and he successfully animated them to convey a feeling of heaviness and slow manoeuvrability. As a result, the spaceship battle sequences look like car chases with supertankers, and when two spacecraft collide, it is like the *Queen Mary* hitting the *Titanic*.

A triumph of digital compositing, *Starship Troopers* combines an amazing number of diverse elements to create a credible interactive environment. In one scene, motion-control (computer-synchronized) cameras were used to match the movements of live actors filmed in front a green screen with the movements of two

Still from 'Starship Troopers' (1997)
During basic training an accident causes the
death of one of Rico's soldiers and he is
whipped as punishment. Here Casper Van Dien
is shaded from the sun before the whipping
begins.

On the set of 'Starship Troopers' (1997)
Casper Van Dien horses around with Paul
Verhoeven.

stop-motion-animated spaceship miniatures as they crashed. Elsewhere, full-scale, fully poseable, hydraulically operated bugs were seamlessly intercut with computer-generated bugs animated using the Digital Input Device. For the scene of an air strike in which the bugs are carpet-bombed along a canyon, writhing and burning CG insects were matched with live-action footage of real explosions to create a mile-long conflagration – the longest rolling explosion in special-effects history. In another scene, CG bugs swarming over a fortress wall were combined with live-action shots such as one of a barrel rolling away after a bug has apparently hit it.

Live-action footage aside, even the combining of purely digital elements was a marvel of engineering and artistry. For the scene where the bugs storm the fortress, Phil Tippett spent sixty hours layering the insects – there are over a thousand bugs in one shot – and animating the swarm so that it moves with credible menace. The special effects for *Starship Troopers* were truly a collective effort, involving a half-dozen different FX studios and hundreds of CG artists, animators, and compositors (including Verhoeven's daughter, Helen). The movie has one of the longest lists of closing credits in history. In terms of the multitudes involved, no wonder Verhoeven has compared the making of this film to building the Notre-Dame cathedral.

While science fiction might have seemed a safe genre far from the risky and provocative subject matter of *Basic Instinct* and *Showgirls*, this movie about kids fighting bugs in outer space ironically proved to be one of Verhoeven's most controversial films. It was accused of being pro-fascist – a gung-ho recruitment film glorifying war. (Critics noted that the film had soldiers firing over 300,000 rounds of ammunition – more than any other movie in history.) Stephen Hunter of the *Washington Post* led the charge, attacking the movie as 'spiritually Nazi, psychologically Nazi. It comes directly out of the Nazi imagination, and is set in the Nazi universe... Unlike films from a civilized society that sees war as a debilitating, tragic necessity... this movie sees it as a profoundly moving experience.'[95] The European press picked up on Hunter's review and bombarded Verhoeven with accusations during his promotional tour for the film: "It was always about me trying to explain what we were trying to do and them saying, 'You're a fucking fascist!' The more fascistic the country had been, the more pissed off they were about the movie."[96] Critics were particularly concerned about how the movie might affect children. Even though it was rated R, the film was marketed with tie-ins that included a TV cartoon series, a computer video game, comic books and toy action figures with accessories such as Johnny's Tactical Nuclear Launcher. As reviewer Dave Kehr wrote, 'What the kids are likely to take away [from *Starship Troopers*] is... a commercialized sense of combat as something glamorous, sexy and rebellious.'[97]

Certainly, the film's lead characters and romantic entanglements are easy for young viewers to identify with: Dizzy wants Johnny who wants Carmen who is wanted by Zander. The film's cast of heartthrobs was in fact chosen from daytime serials (*One Life to Live*, *Days of Our Lives*) and prime-time soap operas (*Beverly Hills 90210*, *Melrose Place*), causing some of the crew to call the film *Melrose Space*. In addition to the flawless faces and perfect bodies of its young leads, the film's utopian world of racial and gender equality has a strong appeal. Witness the group shower scene where male and female recruits are naked together without sexual harassment or even embarrassment. (In actuality, Verhoeven and cinematographer Jost Vacano had to take their own clothes off in order to break the tension for the actors so that they would disrobe and do this co-ed nude scene.) Or consider the

OPPOSITE TOP
On the set of 'Starship Troopers' (1997)
Carmen (front left) becomes a pilot and flies the fleet battle cruiser Rodger Young with Zander Barcalow (Patrick Muldoon, front right). Paul Verhoeven talks the actors through the events that they cannot see so that they react appropriately. The models and explosions are filmed separately and added to the image many months later.

OPPOSITE BOTTOM
Still from 'Starship Troopers' (1997)
The Marshall and Yamamoto battle cruisers collide and explode after being hit by the bug plasma being fired from the planet's surface

"Was it weird doing sequences when the bugs weren't really there?" "No. They described everything that happened and showed it to us in storyboard format. And if all that wasn't working… Paul Verhoeven would gently walk out in front of us and go, 'I'M A 14-FOOT WARRIOR BUG, AND I'M GOING TO KILL YOU! STRIKE! STRIKE!'"

Casper Van Dien

ABOVE
Storyboards for 'Starship Troopers' (1997)
Paul Verhoeven's sketches give a vivid sense of what he wants to achieve. Top Left: The drop ships descend through the bug plasma. Top Right: The drop ships land on Klendathu and the troops mass. This grouping is very similar to the way the bugs are presented (see page 160), so Verhoeven links the roles of the warrior bugs and the ground troops visually. The implication is that, just as there is a hierarchy of men, there is a hierarchy of bugs, so that there is not that much of a difference between the two species. Above Left: Johnny and Dizzy nuke a plasma bug. Above Right: A trooper is caught by a bug.

OPPOSITE TOP
On the set of 'Starship Troopers' (1997)
Verhoeven coaches Casper Van Dien while crew members operate the 'bug sticks'. These sticks enabled the actors to visualise the height, size and position of the bugs to make a more realistic interaction.

OPPOSITE BOTTOM
Still from 'Starship Troopers' (1997)
The finished scene is realistic and frightening. The defeat at Klendathu, where many troops are slaughtered, is used as another reason for the Earth forces to rally and attack the bugs. The number of dead is artificially high because many of the wounded, like Rico, are listed as dead. Implicit in this is that the fascistic Earth powers are using the slaughter as propaganda. The power of Verhoeven's film is the way that the reality and propaganda are both shown, but that the characters never question either, meaning that the viewers have to interpret the film themselves.

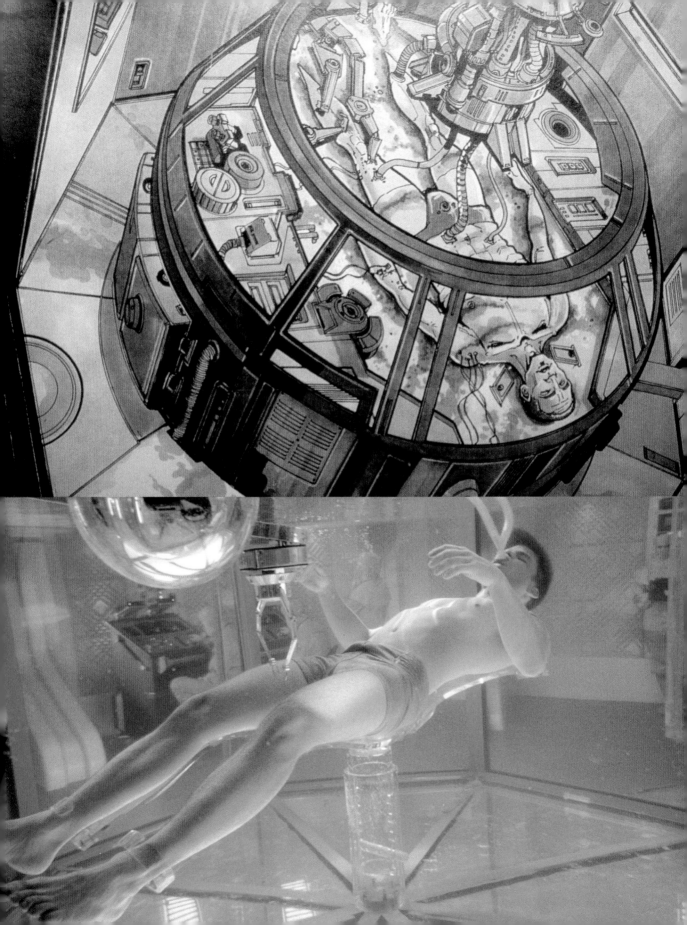

merry-making scene in which both black and white soldiers put the history of slavery behind them and dance to the tune of 'I Wish I Were in Dixie.'

However, with these attractive stars and wonderful society, Verhoeven is slyly setting a trap: "It's subversive, of course. *Starship Troopers* lures you in and then presents you with the bill."[98] Gradually, we begin to realize that all this harmony and equality come at the price of conformity to a military dictatorship. As high school civics teacher Rasczak describes the failure of democracy and the way society was saved from chaos by military rule, and as he goes on to assert that the only true citizens are soldiers, we sense that our young heroes are being seduced into a mindless patriotism and a belief in the warrior ideal. It is then that Verhoeven springs the trap, as these idealistic innocents go off to war and are viciously slaughtered. In unflinchingly graphic battle scenes, humans are stabbed, cut in half and ripped to shreds by the bugs. They are decapitated, dismembered and disemboweled, in shots that had to be trimmed in order to avoid an NC-17 rating. Blood, viscera, amputated limbs and headless trunks are strewn about the battlefield, as in Verhoeven's own childhood memories of seeing the scattered body parts of downed pilots during World War Two. This is war, and Verhoeven presents it with savage realism. One critic described *Starship Troopers* as being 'exactly like *Star Wars* – if you subtract a good story, sympathetic characters, intelligence, wit and moral purpose.'[99] Moral purpose? George Lucas' film, with its comic-book treatment of war as an exciting adventure, is more fascist than Verhoeven's. As Jonathan Rosenbaum has pointed out, 'Wiping out entire planets in the Lucas scheme of things is clean, bloodless, fun that never threatens the camaraderie between fuzzy creatures and humans who trade affectionate wisecracks while zapping enemies from afar.'[100] Verhoeven has contrasted his film with those like *Star Wars*, *Star Trek* and *Independence Day* (1996) where audiences feel safe identifying with invincible heroes: "people *die* in this movie. This isn't one of those comfortable movies where everybody survives."[101] Indeed, though Johnny and Carmen are reunited in the end, their romance is undercut by the fact that most of their comrades have been horribly killed.

Although it is nominally set in the future, *Starship Troopers* is in fact a satiric commentary on the growing militarism and authoritarianism of today's superpowers, particularly the United States. When Johnny is disciplined with a public flogging, the reference is to the American boy who was whipped in Singapore for a minor offence, and to those right-wingers who suggested that such canings should occur in America too as a deterrent to petty crime. When *Starship Troopers'* writer Ed Neumeier (who also scripted *RoboCop*) makes a cameo appearance as a man arrested in the morning, judged in the afternoon and executed that same evening, he is not promoting swift justice or the death penalty. Rather, he has put himself on the line to comment on the dangers of summary judgment and quick consignment to the electric chair. When producer Jon Davison appears as a man who says, "The only good bug is a dead bug," he is there to remind us that the same kind of statement was once made by US forces about the Japanese during World War Two (and before that about Native Americans).

Wartime propaganda always demonizes its enemies in order to justify destroying them. The jingoistic rhetoric ("COUNTDOWN TO VICTORY") and the insecticidal fervour (kids stomping on bugs while their mother applauds hysterically) of the web newscasts in *Starship Troopers* are meant to recall CNN's gung-ho coverage of the Gulf War: "When the Kuwait War started," Verhoeven reminds us,

"When I watched Starship Troopers *I couldn't believe the producers didn't stop Paul Verhoeven. He broke all the rules."*

Takashi Miike

OPPOSITE TOP
Concept painting for 'Starship Troopers' (1997)
A visualisation of Rico in the stasis tank, where his leg is rebuilt after the bug attack. In Verhoeven's Dutch films there is a sense that the central characters are aware that they are capable of evil or cruel acts, but in the American films this element is often missing because of America's self-mythology that it is only capable of doing good (or doing bad things for a good reason). In 'Starship Troopers', the fascistic (essentially American) society is evil, but Verhoeven's ironic presentation of this society was lost on most American viewers.

OPPOSITE BOTTOM
Still from 'Starship Troopers' (1997)
The stasis tank as it appears in the film. Notice the Plexiglas chair under Rico to keep him in position and appear to be floating.

PAGE 158 TOP
Concept painting for 'Starship Troopers' (1997)
When war is declared on the bugs, troops are loaded into drop ships on the battle cruiser Bull Run to attack the planet below. This is a visualisation of the troop-loading scene.

PAGE 158 BOTTOM
On the set of 'Starship Troopers' (1997)
The troop loading is filmed (notice there are now two doors on each ship) several times at different distances and then digitally stitched together against a digital background to give the impression that there are many troops.

PAGE 159 TOP
On the set of 'Starship Troopers' (1997)
Industrial Light & Magic cinematographer Pat Sweeney sets up the motion control camera to film the first time Carmen pilots the Rodger Young. The Rodger Young is a 9-foot-long model and it is coming out of a docking port.

PAGE 159 BOTTOM
Still from 'Starship Troopers' (1997)
The Earth's fleet of battle cruisers comes under attack from bug plasma.

"there was an enormous amount of propaganda in the American media to prepare the American nation for this war. To get the American people behind the government and the war, the USA vilified continuously the other side. The same thing happened when Iraq nearly started again the war. You could read in the newspapers every day again more vilification of Saddam Hussein – true or untrue. The American government is basically about power but the power has strong tendencies to be economic power. It's all opening up markets ultimately. The USA is pretty much aware what opening up markets means for the economy and they are basically using their military presence to open up these markets. It's the same in every country. Hitler did it during World War II."[102] Verhoeven has also noted how certain aspects of his movie turned out to be uncanny predictions of the future: "The whole situation in Afghanistan is almost an exact copy of *Starship Troopers*; the whole gung-ho mentality of bombing everything, blasting the Taliban-forces out of the caves."[103] ("You see a bug hole, you nuke it!") We can only wonder what Verhoeven would make of the 2003 American invasion of Iraq, the lucrative contracts awarded to US companies to 'rebuild' Iraq, and the widespread gloating over Saddam's capture (compare soldiers dragging the Brain Bug out of its hole and their cheering over the fact that "it's afraid"). Could a movie like *Starship Troopers* be made today, in a media climate so saturated by pro-war propaganda and so intolerant of dissent? Verhoeven doesn't think so: "it would be impossible to get it off the ground. The American studios are already asked by the government to be as patriotic as possible and to participate in this 'fight against terrorism.'"[104]Far from being a pro-fascist film, *Starship Troopers* may be the last big-studio movie to throw a wrench into the US propaganda machine.

"You cannot say that our century is getting better for people. It is only getting better in terms of killing. The amount of people that have been killed during the Second World War, or by Stalin, or in Bosnia, or in Indonesia, or in Armenia earlier this century – I mean, look at how people behave when they are unhappy over economic circumstances."

Paul Verhoeven

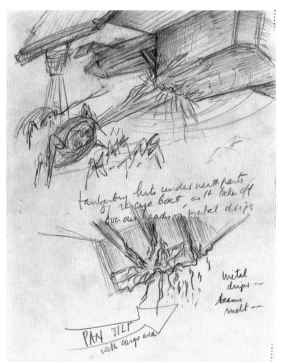

ABOVE
On the set of 'Starship Troopers' (1997)
For close-ups of Denise Richards, various bug legs are positioned around her.

LEFT
Still from 'Starship Troopers' (1997)
The film ends with the capture of a brain bug. Col. Carl Jenkins, now a high-ranking intelligence officer, reads the bug's mind and tells everybody, "It is afraid".

OPPOSITE TOP
Still from 'Starship Troopers' (1997)
A tanker bug can squirt a deadly acid like a flame-thrower. The acid dissolves the troopers, in a shot reminiscent of the famous shot from 'The War of the Worlds' (1953).

OPPOSITE BOTTOM
Storyboards for 'Starship Troopers' (1997)
Verhoeven's sketches show a tanker bug crash through the fortress wall, and spray the aircraft.

TOP
On the set of 'Starship Troopers' (1997)
Phil Tippett, who had worked with Verhoeven on the ED-209 sequence in 'RoboCop', supervised over 200 animation shots for the bugs. The movement of the bugs was achieved using a Digital Input Device, like the one being animated by Animation Supervisor Trey Stokes. The animator moves the puppet, as per traditional model animation, but the actions are recorded to hard disk and then used to move digitally modelled images of the bugs.

ABOVE
On the set of 'Starship Troopers' (1997)
Life-size articulated bugs were made for some close-ups, and cardboard cut-out bugs (shown) were made for rehearsals, so that the actors can see and feel the presence of the bugs. Phil Tippett is the leftmost bug man wearing a white hat.

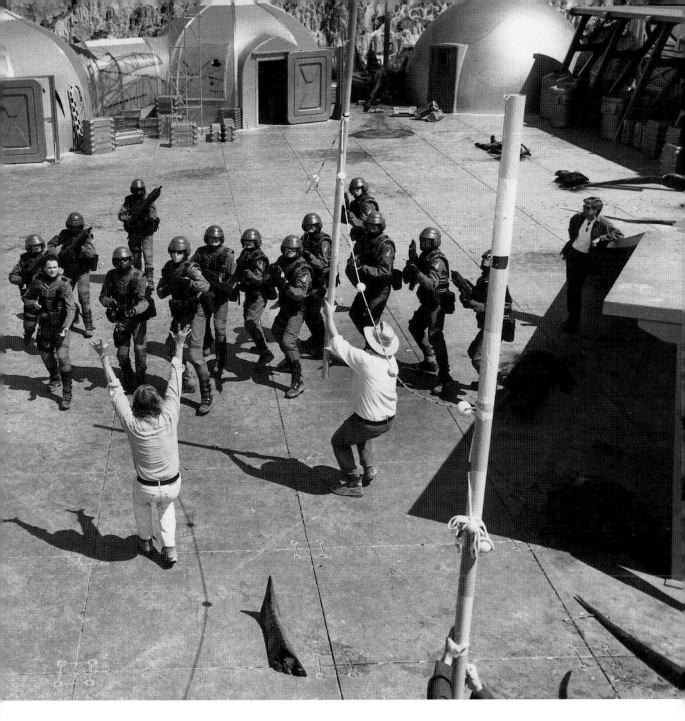

Although *Starship Troopers* was not as big a disappointment at the box office as *Showgirls* had been, it initially returned only about $55 million domestic on its $100 million investment. Perhaps the violence in *Starship Troopers*, like the sex in *Showgirls*, was simply too strong for the American theatrical market. However, just as *Showgirls* did well overseas and gradually gathered a cult following on video, eventually enabling it to turn a profit, so *Starship Troopers* has since become a cult favourite and has earned, when all is said and done, a respectable $121 million worldwide.

On the set of 'Starship Troopers' (1997)
The live shots with actors were filmed first using a motion control camera. Here Paul Verhoeven, centre, helps scare the troopers retreating from the bugs. After the live shots, a 3-D aerial model of the landscape is done, a recreation of the shot is done with no actors so that a blank canvas is captured and shots of a large grey sphere are taken to measure the light source. All this information was used to fully integrate the animated bugs into the landscape.

Still from 'Hollow Man' (2000)
A group of government scientists in a secret underground bunker have discovered how to make living things invisible, but they do not know how to make them visible again. They experiment with a new formula and are able to bring back a gorilla to visibility.

Verhoeven was now somewhat at risk of being thought an unbankable director, so he toned down both the sex and the violence on his next project, *Hollow Man* (2000), in a deliberate decision to make a more conventionally commercial blockbuster. As Verhoeven has said about making Hollywood movies, "I think you are part of a system. You have to acknowledge that it is not only art. Like building a house where we cannot live. Skyscrapers look absolutely great from the outside, but [what if] there is no toilet! Or something like that. And for a 90 million dollar movie, you need an audience. Otherwise it collapses."[105] *Hollow Man* was the first movie that Verhoeven did not have to recut and resubmit over and over again to the MPAA to receive an R rating; it got one right away. The calculation worked, and *Hollow Man* became Verhoeven's biggest hit since *Basic Instinct*, grossing $73 million in the US and $180 million worldwide. Nearly $50 million of the film's budget was earmarked for special effects and, as usual with a Verhoeven film, they

were state of the art. The director had originally thought that shooting *Hollow Man* would not be terribly challenging. Like the bugs in *Starship Troopers*, the 'invisible man' effects would just be digitally added in post-production, and Kevin Bacon, who plays that role, would not have to be on the set except for 30% of the time when his character is visible. However, what Verhoeven soon realized is that without Bacon there to interact with physically and psychologically, the other actors were stranded in empty space, and the scenes looked stiff, inorganic and unconvincing. They did not live up to Verhoeven's exacting sense of realism. So it was decided that Bacon would act in all his character's scenes, even the ones where he would later be made to look invisible, so that "when there are physical interactions between characters," Verhoeven says, "it looks real because we really did it! When Sebastian [Bacon's character] is grabbing someone's clothes or pushing them around, they react realistically because Kevin was really doing it!"[106] But this meant that, rather than

TOP
On the set of 'Hollow Man' (2000)
There are problems with the reversion process and the gorilla needs to be shocked back to life. Here Paul Verhoeven goes through the actions with Elizabeth Shue. The supports under the shock paddles are coated in green and will be digitally removed.

ABOVE
On the set of 'Hollow Man' (2000)
Here Verhoeven instructs the gorilla (actually Tom Woodruff, Jr.).

Still from 'Hollow Man' (2000)

Project leader and genius Sebastian Caine (Kevin Bacon) decides to try the invisibility formula on himself, so that he will be the first human being to be invisible. He writhes in agony. The outer layer of his skin disappears to show the bone and muscle tissue below. Bacon's body was scanned and a computer model created that included every bone, muscle and organ in his body, pushing the limits of special effects technology.

adding an invisible Bacon to the scenes, he had to be digitally removed to create the impression of his absence. Of course, this left holes that had to be filled in with the backgrounds that should be visible if we are able to see through the invisible man, which in turn meant that each scene had to be filmed twice, once with the actors and then again without them to get the backgrounds to be seen 'through' Bacon. Thus two passes of each scene were made using a motion-control camera so that the camera movements each time would be exactly alike, and these were then digitally composited to give us the effect of transparency.

But that's not all, for Verhoeven also wanted special effects that would suggest Bacon's presence in spite of his invisibility. Since *Hollow Man* is a ghost thriller and not a comedy, floating pencils and bobbing shirts were to be avoided. Instead, Bacon would be creepily outlined in such substances as smoke, water and blood. In acting these scenes, Bacon had to wear a latex body suit, a face mask, contact lenses, and a dental plate that were all one colour – green for blood, blue for smoke, and black for water. Visual effects supervisor Craig Hayes would then replace the coloured Bacon with a digital clone so that we would see, for example, pool water or raindrops form a pantomime outline of him performing. In order to make this 'water man' look and move as much like Bacon as possible, information about every aspect of the actor's body, down to the thickness of his fingernails and how his mouth would look in a smile, was scanned into a computer to create a three-dimensional model of his appearance and actions. In a sense, then, the special effects in *Hollow Man* never lose touch with the actor, remaining rooted in his body, for

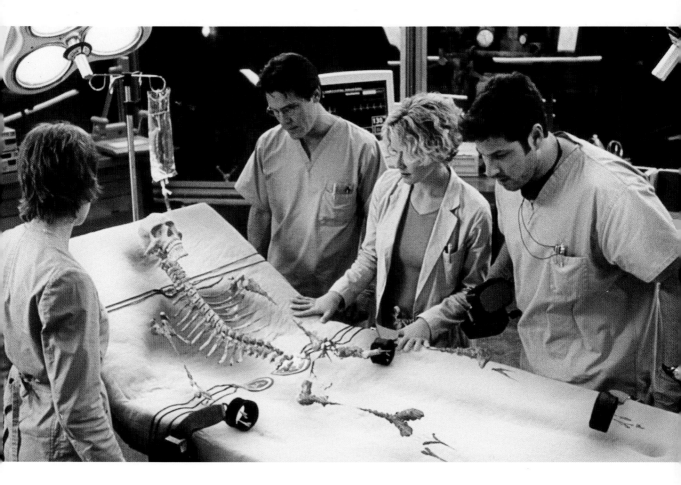

Still from 'Hollow Man' (2000)
Sebastian loses consciousness just before he
disappears entirely.

the computer clone that 'replaces' Bacon is a digital translation of his own physical movements and facial expressions.

Yet Verhoeven wanted still more from his FX crew. During the transformation scene where Bacon becomes invisible, he doesn't disappear all at once but in stages, with the skin the first to go, then the writhing muscles, the heaving lungs, the pounding heart and finally the skeleton. Verhoeven's daughter Helen saw the *écorchés* (wax replicas of bodies with their internal organs visible) at the Museo della Specola anatomy museum in Italy and bought illustrated books on the subject for her father. Inspired by these, Verhoeven asked special effects supervisor Scott Anderson to create a three-dimensional digital model of the *inside* of Bacon's body, with all his organs working and muscles flexing as they do in real life. Because this model included different layers of innards moving each on top of the other, it was about twenty times more complex than animating dinosaurs where only surfaces were involved. Special volume-rendering software had to be developed, using vast amounts of computer memory, to render a true replica of the body's insides. When Verhoeven was asked why he was so insistent on having anatomically correct, fully functioning innards for the in-between states of Bacon's transformation to invisibility, the director answered, "I feel that if I made it really realistic, they would have to accept... invisibility. ...I thought if I made the transitions as good as possible, and you can really see all the veins that are there, then I can sell the bluff better."[107] Variously described by critics as stunning, beautiful and nauseating ('who, exactly, apart from ghouls and third-year medical students, wants to see it?'),[108] these

Still from 'Hollow Man' (2000)
When Kevin Bacon read the script he thought that he would not have to do much work because he was invisible for 75% of the time. However, he was also required for all the invisible scenes.

viscera-revealing transformation scenes are among the most memorable special effects in any movie.

For the actor whose every body part, including his genitals, had to be scanned into the computer, and who had to wear spray-painted, skin-tight leotards and a mask glued to his face during much of the shoot, the role of 'invisible man' was arduous and uncomfortable, as Kevin Bacon has detailed in a diary he kept during filming. While Guy Pearce and Edward Norton were also considered for the role, Verhoeven chose Bacon for his ability to be both charming and diabolical, but also for his willingness to undergo pain. As Bacon has noted, his first meeting with Verhoeven about the role was strange in that the director spent only five minutes talking about the character, but fifty-five minutes talking about the suffering the role would entail. Even this, Bacon says, did not adequately prepare him for the wear and tear on his skin and other pains he experienced. But the sense of isolation, anger and suffering he felt in that mask and body suit did, he believes, help his performance in the part. Verhoeven had nothing but praise for Bacon's uncomplaining attitude and game performance: "Some actors are like horses, galloping until they can't stop anymore. Kevin Bacon is an actor who will go on and on and on until he can't go anymore."[109]

In *Hollow Man*, Bacon plays Sebastian Caine, a cocky scientist who goes power-mad when invisibility allows him to rape and murder with impunity. Verhoeven has noted that the idea of a megalomaniacal invisible man can be found in the second book of Plato's *Republic*: "Plato says man is not just and decent because of internal morals; [rather,] he is obedient to the restraints of society. If you remove those restraints – if a man were to become invisible – he would steal whatever he could get, enter every house, rape every woman, kill all the men and basically behave like a god."[110] As Verhoeven's preferred movie tagline put it: 'What would you do if you knew you couldn't be seen?' (The tagline used was: 'Think you're alone? Think again.') The film encourages us to identify with the clever and charismatic Sebastian, and the camera often adopts his point of view as the invisible man, tempting us to become voyeurs along with him, to get off on our ability to see without being seen, to take whatever and whomever we want. According to Verhoeven, "*Hollow Man* leads you by the hand and takes you with Sebastian into teasing behaviour, naughty behaviour, and then really bad and ultimately evil behaviour. At what point do you abandon him? I'm thinking when he rapes the woman would probably be the moment that people decide, 'This is not exactly my type of hero', though I must say a lot of viewers follow him further than you would expect."[111]

The scene where Sebastian as the invisible man rapes the woman in a neighbouring apartment was shot two ways. The second shot shows the terrified woman screaming as she is being raped. However, preview audiences thought the scene was too painful and that it alienated them too soon from Sebastian's character. Verhoeven trimmed it back: "So we changed it, but in the case of the rape, the original version in my opinion was stronger and harsher and at the same time was more relevant for the character of Sebastian Caine than the more elliptic one that finally ended up in the movie."[112] Some reviewers have criticized Verhoeven for making these cuts in the rape scene, arguing that he compromised his vision, eradicated the confrontational elements of his previous films, and flinched from showing Sebastian's sexual violence. However, it should be noted that Verhoeven never intended to show the rape itself, for to do so in this particular case would actually have made it look *less* realistic: "Strangely enough, a woman being raped by

an invisible man would look silly and that's the last thing we'd want to do. Even
with all the greatest special effects in the world, people would think it was funny. It
wouldn't express in any way the severity of the violence happening at that
moment."[113] It should also be said that when it comes to showing sex and violence
on screen, Verhoeven just can't win with the critics, being damned if he does and
damned if he doesn't: "American critics always complain about the blandness of
mainstream movies, but when you do something more ambiguous and ironic, they
are pissed off too. ...The irony is that when *Starship Troopers* came out, the
American critics condemned it. But now, three years later, they're saying: 'How
could the director of such an interesting, multi-layered film as *Starship Troopers*
make a simplistic piece of shit like *Hollow Man*?'"[114]

Hollow Man is less simplistic if seen as Verhoeven's most recent meditation on
corporeality. Sebastian's becoming invisible in the transformation scene is painful in
the extreme, involving writhing limbs and a nearly exploding heart, as if the loss of
visible presence were somehow a violence done to the body, a disintegration of it
layer by layer – skin, muscles, heart and bone. It is interesting that in commenting
on the transformation scene, Verhoeven has said, "There is a lot of opening of the
human body in my movies, a lot of deterioration of the human body, falling apart.

Still from 'Hollow Man' (2000)
Linda McKay (Elisabeth Shue) and Sebastian
Caine used to be lovers, but Sebastian's ego and
drive to succeed drove them apart. When he
becomes invisible, Sebastian feels he has power
over people, and desires Linda again. To give
him some sort of presence, Linda makes a mask
for him to wear.

ABOVE
On the set of 'Hollow Man' (2000)
Paul Verhoeven lines up the characters. Virtually every shot is a special effects shot that requires a motion control camera. As in 'Starship Troopers', once the actors have been filmed the background is filmed as well, using the exact same camera movements. If there are any other elements to be added, like water or smoke, then these are filmed so that they can be layered into the final image. In this picture, Kevin Bacon has taken off his green gloves between takes.

PAGE 174 TOP
On the set of 'Hollow Man' (2000)
Verhoeven talks through the storyboards with cinematographer Jost Vacano (centre). The storyboards have to be followed because this is what the special effects people have agreed to and budgeted for. It also makes it quicker to film. If Paul wanted to change a sequence, then it could cost anything up to $300,000 for the special effects team to do it.

PAGE 174 BOTTOM
On the set of 'Hollow Man' (2000)
Paul Verhoeven makes some additional notes for himself.

"I was playing a mad scientist so it helped that my director was one as well 'cause I had something to base my character on."

Kevin Bacon

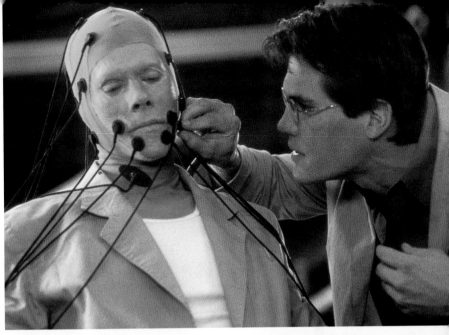

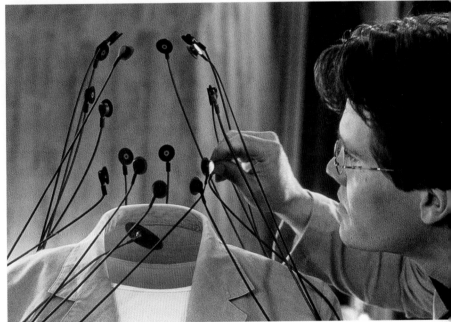

PAGE 175 TOP
On the set of 'Hollow Man' (2000)
After working together for 25 years Vacano and Verhoeven do not talk with words, they talk with images. Here Verhoeven lines up an image and moves around the set with Vacano following every nuance. Vacano began working on documentaries before lensing films like 'The Lost Honor of Katherine Blum' (1975) and 'Das Boot' (1981) as well as seven films for Verhoeven.

PAGE 175 BOTTOM
On the set of 'Hollow Man' (2000)
Verhoeven is always active on the set, happy to pick up props and show the actions to the actors, or to run down the street with the stuntman, as in this image. The stuntman is doubling Kevin Bacon, and is wearing a black costume because it absorbs light. For scenes with water and reflective surfaces a green costume would have made green reflections whereas a black costume disappears into the background and can be filled in with special effects if necessary.

TOP
On the set of 'Hollow Man' (2000)
Matthew Kensington (Josh Brolin) places electrodes on Sebastian. Kevin Bacon's green make-up, green contact lens and green costume will be digitally removed. His presence allows the other actors to interact with him.

ABOVE
Still from 'Hollow Man' (2000)
With Bacon removed from the image, the electrodes on him remain and can be used on the image. However, the electrodes we cannot see at the back of his head have to be added, and also we have to see the back of his clothes.

I'm very sensitive to the weakness and the vulnerability of the human body."[115] Once he has become invisible and 'disembodied', Sebastian feels invulnerable and starts to prey on others, believing that he can do so with impunity. It is as if there's some fundamental connection between physical embodiment and morality. A person who seems to have no body that can be injured recognizes no fear or pain-boundary when it comes to injuring others and, feeling himself invincible, loses empathy with others whose bodies are vulnerable. The invisible Sebastian penetrates other bodies – as when he rapes a woman or impales a man – as if he were trying to prove his superiority to others' bodily weakness, to defy them or God to injure him. In the end, he gets what may be his deepest wish, for he is finally beaten and burned back into visible presence, and reminded, as he dies, that he too has a mortal body. In injury and death, there is an end to his isolation, for he can now join the rest of humanity.

On the set of 'Hollow Man' (2000)
Plato once hypothesized that if a man were invisible and could do anything then he would act like an evil god. Well, Sebastian does not disappoint. He traps his fellow scientists in the underground laboratory and kills them off one by one. Here Verhoeven feels the gut-wrenching pain after Frank Chase (Joey Slotnick) is attacked by Sebastian.

Over the years, Verhoeven has discussed many possible future film projects with varying degrees of seriousness and plausibility. Somewhat facetiously, he once considered doing a sequel to *Showgirls* to be called *Bimbos: Nomi Goes Hollywood* – presumably an exposé of Tinseltown to rival that of Sin City. The possibility of a *Basic Instinct 2* has also been raised, but only if Verhoeven and Sharon Stone can get beyond their rancorous disagreement over whether the director forewarned the star about how much of her would be revealed in the leg-uncrossing scene. A further *RoboCop* has come up for discussion, this one to be the first real sequel in that it would bring Peter Weller back in the title role, and it would provide satirical commentary on recent economic, military and political trends in America – that is, if it is still possible for a Dutch-born director to make a Hollywood movie that is critical of the US. As Verhoeven has said, "I'm the outsider, and that is what has provoked the negativism towards my work, and the personal attacks. Because somehow they look at me like they did at the Commies in the 1950s – they see danger, and they want to know what I'm doing here."[116]

Verhoeven's critical fearlessness is apparent from a plan that he and Bobby Shriver (Arnold Schwarzenegger's brother-in-law) once had to make a film about Hitler's rise to power as an implied parallel to Reagan's: "The idea would be to show that charisma is not identical with good. So basically you would see how a charismatic person would be able to seduce 50 or 60 million Germans. And I think Bobby was also looking at American politics, probably at the Reagan period, to make a point through another piece in another time."[117] Another controversial project, with Schwarzenegger as the star, would have been a film about the Crusades, which Verhoeven planned to depict with brutal realism as a "murderous attack of the Christians on the Arabs and the Jews. The Pope instigates this complete slaughter."[118] A more positive – though still realistic – view of Christianity was to be presented in a film about the life of Christ, based on the historical research of theologians in the Jesus Seminar. "I feel it's nonsense to do another movie on the mythic Jesus," Verhoeven has said; "I want to know what's true."[119] While a movie about *Christ, the Man* (its tentative title) would be a risky undertaking ("That's a dangerous project – beyond the critics, it's physically dangerous, as we know from the people who shoot abortion doctors"),[120] Verhoeven's interest in the Jesus biopic has been strong enough to keep the project alive for many years, and even to 'advertise' it in *Showgirls* with a neon sign that says, "Jesus Is Coming Soon."

LEFT
On the set of 'Hollow Man' (2000)
Although Sebastian may feel he is a god, he is still made of flesh and blood, even if we cannot see it. In one sequence Linda defends herself using a makeshift flame-thrower. Verhoeven walks Elizabeth Shue (behind him) through the movements of this dangerous part of the film-making process.

BELOW
Still from 'Hollow Man' (2000)
Linda in action.

Still from 'Hollow Man' (2000)
Sebastian is invisible but the scientists find ways to make him visible so that they can fight him. Trapped in the medical supply room, Sarah Kennedy (Kim Dickens) throws packets of blood over Sebastian and they wrestle for control of the tranquiliser gun.

Two female biopics in development by Verhoeven show his continuing interest in movies featuring strong women. In the first, Nicole Kidman would star as nineteenth-century feminist Victoria Woodhull, a suffragette and free-love advocate. Its tentative title is *The Prostitute Who Ran for President.* The second biopic would be about Leni Riefenstahl, director of such aesthetically brilliant but pro-Nazi propaganda films as *Triumph of the Will* (1935). Jodie Foster had been mentioned for the lead role, but as Verhoeven told *Time* magazine, Riefenstahl herself balked at this choice, saying that "'Jodie's not beautiful enough to play me.' ...Leni's ultimate idea of herself is Sharon Stone in *Basic Instinct.*"[121]

Most recently, Verhoeven has reteamed with Gerard Soeteman, the screenwriter on all of his earlier Dutch films, to develop three projects that show the most promise of seeing the light of day as finished films. *Azazel* ('Scapegoat'), based on a book by popular Russian author Boris Akunin, is about a young detective in 1876 St. Petersburg who investigates a series of apparent suicides and ends up taking on terrorists who will later murder the Czar and start the Russian Revolution. Verhoeven has described the main character as a cross between Sherlock Holmes and Indiana Jones. *Batavia's Graveyard* is the true story of a seventeenth-century Dutch ship which runs aground on a coral reef off the coast of Western Australia. The shipwrecked survivors end up forming a fascist regime which splits into two rival factions at each other's throats. Verhoeven has called the film a real-life *Lord of the Flies* but with adults. Finally, as this book goes to press, Verhoeven announced

that he would be shooting *Zwartboek* ('Black Book'), a thriller set in the final months of World War Two and featuring a Dutch female heroine. Verhoeven has described his current goal as that of making films in Europe using American actors so that the movies will be able to compete on the international market.

Certainly, whatever Verhoeven does next will push back boundaries and confound expectations: "I'm overreaching, I'm always trying to get things that are beyond my possibilities. I always push the limits. I try to do things that I have not done before, that are dangerous, overwhelming and challenging."[122] "I like controversy," Verhoeven admits; "It has always been inspiring to me... to say, 'Fuck it, [If] nobody thinks I am going to shoot it, I'll shoot it'"[123]

Still from 'Hollow Man' (2000)
As Matthew and Linda attempt to leave, Sebastian is shown outlined in the water from the sprinkler system. This was achieved by blending Kevin Bacon's performance (his body language) and the computer model of him.

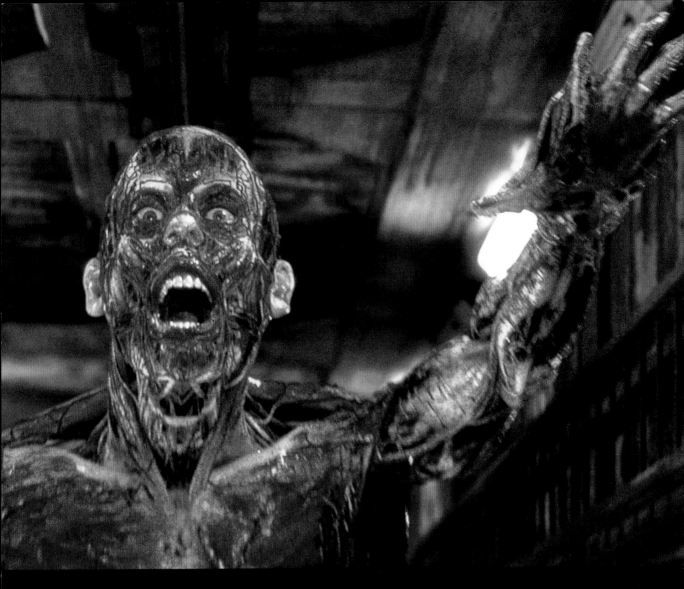

OPPOSITE
On the set of 'Hollow Man' (2000)
The terrifying climax takes place in the elevator shaft to the surface. As Linda breaks free of Sebastian he falls into the literal abyss (an abyss he has inhabited mentally for some time). Here a stunt-man falls.

ABOVE
Still from 'Hollow Man' (2000)
And here is Sebastian falling to his death, in a shot not unlike the climax of Alfred Hitchcock's 'Saboteur' (1942), when Norman Lloyd falls off the Statue of Liberty.

"Paul thinks – and I think he's right in a certain way – that the dark characters are much more interesting. He's much more for the dark underground, to see what's beneath the surface."

Jost Vacano

Zwartboek

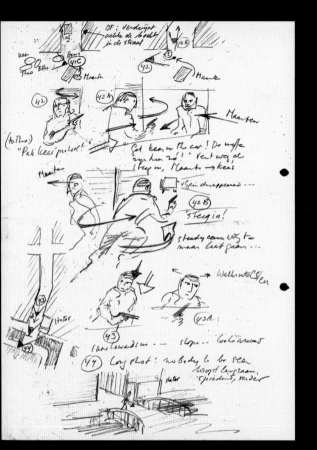

Script pages for 'Zwartboek' (2005)
At the time of writing Paul Verhoeven is waiting to find additional financing before filming can begin on 'Zwartboek'. The story is a World War Two revenge thriller about a young Jewish woman who works for the Dutch Resistance while apparently collaborating with the Nazis. It will be filmed in the Netherlands, representing Verhoeven's first return there since 'The Fourth Man' (1983), and his first collaboration with

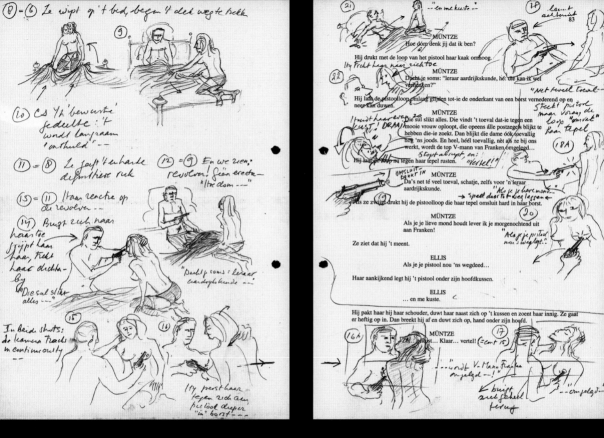

Script pages for 'Zwartboek' (2005)
In this scene the central character Ellis has a
sexual liaison with Müntze, but what she takes to

Chronology

ABOVE
Paul Verhoeven (c1940)

RIGHT
Paul Verhoeven (1964)
Paul becomes a Lieutenant-3rd Class in the Dutch Navy.

1938 Paul Verhoeven is born on 18 July, to Wim and Nel Verhoeven in Amsterdam, the Netherlands. His father is a primary school teacher and headmaster.

1940 The Germans invade the Netherlands, and between the ages of two and seven, the young Verhoeven witnesses summary executions of Dutch people by their Nazi occupiers, and Allied planes bombing and being shot down close to where he and his parents live.

1955 Attends art school in Paris, where he is influenced by the unflinching realism of Dutch paintings by Rembrandt and Hieronymus Bosch. Misses the deadline to apply for film school in Paris.

1956 Attends the University of Leiden in the Netherlands, where he joins the elite Leiden Student Association and is subjected to humiliating hazing rituals like those he later depicts in *Soldier of Orange*. Joins the Leiden film club and sees movies by directors who will have a lasting influence on his own work: Ingmar Bergman, Billy Wilder, Akira Kurosawa, David Lean, Federico Fellini, Orson Welles and most importantly, Alfred Hitchcock.

1960 Directs his first film, a 35-minute short called *One Lizard Too Many* (*Een Hagedis Teveel*), inspired by Alain Renais' *Hiroshima Mon Amour*. Directs three more short films over the next three years.

1964 Earns a Ph.D. in mathematics and physics, with a special interest in Einstein's Theory of Relativity. Is drafted into the military, and manages to get himself assigned to the Marine Film Service.

1965 Directs his first large-scale action film and his first movie in colour, *The Marine Corps* (*Het Korps Mariniers*), a documentary celebrating the tercentenary of the Dutch Marine Corps. Cuts his teeth on directing battle scenes, similar to those that will later figure in *Soldier of Orange* and *Starship Troopers*.

1966 Has mental crisis due to his girlfriend's unplanned pregnancy, religious scruples concerning abortion, and how the responsibilities of fatherhood might cut short his career as a film director. They decide to have the abortion.

1967 Marries his girlfriend, Martine Tours, a psychologist, on 7 April. Martine became a violinist when she went to the United States.

1968 Directs a television documentary about the leader of the Dutch fascist party, *Portrait of Anton Adriaan Mussert*, which, due to political controversy, does not air until 1970. Directs *Floris*, a family-oriented TV series about a kind of Dutch Ivanhoe or Robin Hood, which becomes Verhoeven's first project with star Rutger Hauer and writer Gerard Soeteman.

1970 Directs a short sex comedy, *The Wrestler* (*De Worstelaar*), which is Verhoeven's first work with cinematographer Jan de Bont.

1971 Directs *Business Is Business* (a.k.a. *Any Special Way*, *Wat Zien Ik*), Verhoeven's first full-length feature, a sex comedy about the lives of female prostitutes in Amsterdam's red-light district.

1973 Directs *Turkish Fruit* (*Turks Fruit*), a tragic love story that proves to be a tremendous hit in the Netherlands – it is still the highest-grossing Dutch film ever made. Nominated for an Academy Award as Best Foreign Film. Rutger Hauer's big-screen debut.

1975 Directs *Katie Tippel* (*Keetje Tippel*), a costume drama, at a cost of almost a million dollars – then the most expensive Dutch movie ever made.

1977 Directs *Soldier of Orange* (*Soldaat van Oranje*), a World War Two drama, which becomes Verhoeven's international breakthrough hit. The film wins both the Golden Globe Award and the Los Angeles Film Critics' Award for Best Foreign Film.

1980 Prompted by an admiring Steven Spielberg, Verhoeven visits Hollywood and enters into discussions with studio executives that lay the groundwork for his later career of making movies in America. Back in the Netherlands, Verhoeven has trouble getting a government subsidy for the controversial social-realist film, *Spetters*. To secure financing, he agrees to cut the script, but then directs the uncensored version of the script anyway.

Spetters becomes a *succès de scandale*, with theaters picketed by groups claiming that the film is anti-woman, anti-gay and anti-disabled.

1983   Directs *The Fourth Man* (*De Vierde Man*), a film noir with a gay twist which has success on the international art-house circuit. The film wins the Los Angeles Film Critics' Award for Best Foreign Film.

1985   Directs the medieval epic *Flesh+Blood* (a.k.a. *The Rose and the Sword*), Verhoeven's first film with an international cast, crew, and funding, and his first movie made outside of his native Netherlands (it is filmed in Spain). Finally, weary of struggling to maintain creative control while trying to secure financing, particularly from the Dutch government subsidy board, Verhoeven journeys to Hollywood on 28 September.

1986   Verhoeven's first directing job in Hollywood is an episode of the HBO cable TV series, *The Hitchhiker*. Verhoeven joins the Jesus Seminar, a group of progressive theologians who gather yearly to discuss the historical roots of Christ.

1987   Directs *RoboCop*, which becomes the sleeper hit of the summer, shooting up to number one on *Variety*'s Movie Top Ten list. Verhoeven's first feature film made in Hollywood is the one that secures his reputation as a bankable director.

1990   Trying his hand at another science-fiction film after *RoboCop*, Verhoeven directs *Total Recall* with star Arnold Schwarzenegger, which becomes an even bigger hit. Verhoeven gets listed as number 50 on *Premiere* magazine's list of the 100 most powerful people in Hollywood.

1992   Directs the Hitchcockian erotic thriller *Basic Instinct*, with Sharon Stone in the controversial role of a bisexual femme fatale. Gay protests disrupt filming in San Francisco and raise awareness about homophobia, but also help the film to become a *succès de scandale*. Stone and Verhoeven have a public dispute over whether she had authorized him to reveal so much of her in the leg-uncrossing scene.

1995   Directs the revealing Vegas musical *Showgirls*, becoming the first director in history to get pre-approval from a major Hollywood studio to make a big-budget NC-17 movie. The film is Verhoeven's first box-office flop, but then goes on to success as a cult film on the midnight-movie circuit and on video. Verhoeven 'wins' a Golden Raspberry Award and becomes the first director in history to attend the Razzies ceremony and personally accept his prize for Worst Director.

1997   Returning to science fiction, Verhoeven directs *Starship Troopers*, which provokes controversy over its politics, with some seeing it as pro-fascist and others viewing it as a satire on gung-ho militarism.

1999   *Turkish Delight* is voted Best Dutch Film of the Century at the Netherlands Film Festival.

2000   Directs *Hollow Man*, starring Kevin Bacon as a sex-crazed and power-mad scientist.

2005   Scheduled to direct *Black Book* (*Zwartboek*), Verhoeven's first Dutch-based movie since 1983.

LEFT
7 April 1967, Wedding
Martine Tours marries Paul Verhoeven.

ABOVE
28 April 1995, Los Angeles
Martine looks on as Paul receives a knighthood from Mattie Peters, the Consul General of the Netherlands.

Filmography

One Lizard Too Many
(Een Hagedis Teveel, 1960)
Crew: *Director* Paul Verhoeven, *Writer* Jan van Mastrigt, *Music* Aart Gisolf, *Cinematographer* Frits Boersma, *Editor* Ernst Winar, B&W, 35 minutes.
Cast: Erik Bree, Marijke Jones, Hermine Menalda, Hans Schneider.

Nothing Special *(Niets Bijzonders, 1961)*
Crew: *Director* Paul Verhoeven, *Writer* Jan van Mastrigt, *Cinematographer* Frits Boersma, B&W, 9 minutes.
Cast: Jan van Mastrigt, Marina Schapers.

The Hitchhikers *(De Lifters, 1962)*
Crew: *Director* Paul Verhoeven, *Writer* Jan van Mastrigt, *Cinematographer* Frits Boersma, *Editor* Ernst Winar, B&W, 17 minutes.
Cast: Geerda Walma van der Molen, Jaap van Donselaar, Maarten Schutte, Jan van Mastrigt.

Let's Have a Party *(Feest, 1963)*
Crew: *Director & Producer* Paul Verhoeven, *Writer* Jan van Mastrigt, *Music* Dick Broeckaerts, *Cinematographer* Ferenc Kalman-Gall, *Editor* Ernst Winar, B&W, 28 minutes.
Cast: Yvonne Blei-Weissmann, Dick de Brauw, Pieter Jelle Bouman, Wim Noordhoek.

The Marine Corps
(Het Korps Mariniers, 1965)
Crew: *Director* Paul Verhoeven, *Music* H. C. van Lijnschoten, *Cinematographers* Peter Alsemgeest, Jan Kijser & Jos van Haarlem, *Editor* Ernst Winar, Colour, 23 minutes.

Portrait of Anton Adriaan Mussert
(Portret van Anton Adriaan Mussert, 1968)
Crew: *Director* Paul Verhoeven, *Compilers* Paul Verhoeven, Leo Kool & Hans Keller, *Commentary* Hans Keller, *Cinematographer* Jaap Buis, B&W, 50 minutes.

Floris *(1969)*
Crew: *Director* Paul Verhoeven, *Writer* Gerard Soeteman, *Producer* Max Appelboom, *Music* Julius Staffaro, *Cinematographer* Ton Bune, *Editor* Jan Bosdriesz, B&W, 12 episodes, 30 minutes per episode.
Cast: Rutger Hauer (Floris van Rosemondt), Jos Bergman (Sindala), Hans Culeman (Maarten van Rossem), Diana Marlet (Gravin Ada), Ida Bons (Viola), Tim Beekman (Sergeant), Ton Vos (Wolter van Odesteijn), Hans Kemna (Govert), Henk van Ulsen, Hans Boskamp (Lange Pier), Hammy de Beukalaer.

The Wrestler *(De Worstelaar, 1970)*
Crew: *Director* Paul Verhoeven, *Writers* Paul Verhoeven & Kees Holierhoek, *Producer* Nico Crama, *Music* J Stoeckart, *Cinematographer* Jan de Bont, *Editor* Jan Bosdriesz, Colour, 20 minutes.
Cast: Jon Bluming, Bernhard Droog, Wim Zomer, Marielle Fiolet.

Business Is Business
(Any Special Way, Wat Zien Ik?, 1971)
Crew: *Director* Paul Verhoeven, *Writer* Gerard Soeteman, *Short Stories* Albert Mol, *Producer* Rob Houwer, *Music* Julius Steffaro, *Cinematographer* Jan de Bont, *Editor* Jan Bosdriesz, Colour, 93 minutes.

Cast: Ronny Bierman (Blonde Greet), Sylvia de Leur (Nel), Piet Romer (Greet's Lover), Bernhard Droog (Nel's Husband), Henk Molenberg (Greet's Customer, Cleaning Scenes), Albert Mol (Blind Date), Jules Hamel (Nel's Pimp), Eric van Ingen (Greet's Customer, Doctor Scene), Trudy Labij (Prostitute), Ton Lensink (Greet's Customer, Witch Scene), Dini de Neef (Older Prostitute), Carry Tefsen (Prostitute), Andre van den Heuvel (Drunken Pub-Crawler), Allard van der Scheer (Greet's Customer, School Scene), Helmet Woudenberg (Greet's Customer, First One), Jan Verhoeven (Greet's Customer, Chicken Scene).

Turkish Delight *(Turks Fruit, 1973)*
Crew: *Director* Paul Verhoeven, *Writer* Gerard Soeteman, *Novel* Jan Wolkers, *Executive Producer* Rob Houwer, *Music* Rogier van Otterloo, *Cinematographer* Jan de Bont, *Editor* Jan Bosdriesz, *Art Director* Ralf van de Elst, Colour, 112 minutes.
Cast: Monique van de Ven (Olga Stapels), Rutger Hauer (Erik Vonk), Tonny Huurdeman (Mother), Wim van den Brink (Father), Hans Boskamp (Shop Manager), Dolf de Vries (Paul), Manfred de Graaf (Henny), Dick Scheffer (Accountant), Marjol Flore (Tineke), Marijke Frijlink (Moniek), Olga Zuiderhoek (Gonnie), Maartje Seyferth (Josje), Aime Mars (Indonesian Girl), Suzie Broks (Truus), Jaap van Donselaar & Hans Kemna (Eric's Friends).

Katie Tippel *(Keetje Tippel, 1975)*
Crew: *Director* Paul Verhoeven, *Writer* Gerard Soeteman, *Memoirs* Neel Doff, *Executive Producer* Rob Houwer, *Music* Rogier van Otterloo, *Cinematographer* Jan de Bont, *Editor*

Jane Sperr, *Art Director* Roland de Groot, *Costumes* Robert Bos, Colour, 109 minutes.
Cast: Monique van de Ven (Keetje Tippel), Rutger Hauer (Hugo), Peter Faber (George), Eddy Brugman (Andre), Hannah de Leeuwe (Mina, Keetje's Sister), Andrea Domburg (Keetje's Mother), Jan Blaaser (Keetje's Father), Huib Broos (Manager of Wax Factory), Theu Boermans (Doctor), Carry Tefsen (Woman in Wax Factory).

Soldier of Orange
(Soldaat van Oranje, 1977)
Crew: *Director* Paul Verhoeven, *Writers* Gerard Soeteman, Kees Holierhoek & Paul Verhoeven, *Novel* Erik Hazelhoff Roelfzema, *Producer* Rob Houwer, *Music* Rogier van Otterloo, *Cinematographer* Jost Vacano, *Editor* Jane Sperr, *Art Director* Roland de Groot, Colour, 153 minutes.
Cast: Rutger Hauer (Erik Lanshof), Jeroen Krabbé (Guus LeJeune), Susan Penhaligon (Susan), Edward Fox (Colonel Rafelli), Lex van Delden (Nico), Derek de Lint (Alex), Huib Rooymans (John Weinberg), Dolf de Vries (Jack Ten Brinck), Eddy Habbema (Robby), Belinda Meuldijk (Esther), Peter Faber (Will), Rijk de Gooyer (Gestapo-Man Breitner), Reinhard Kolldehoff (Geisman), Andrea Domburg (Queen Wilhelmina), Guus Hermus (Van der Zanden).

Gone, Gone *(Voorbij, Voorbij, 1979)*
Crew: *Director* Paul Verhoeven, *Writer* Gerard Soeteman, *Producer* Joop van den Ende, *Music* Hans Vermeulen, *Cinematographer* Mat van Hensbergen, *Editor* Ine Schenkkan, Colour, 58 minutes.

Cast: Andre van den Heuvel (Ab), Andrea Domburg (Dorien), Piet Romer (Gerben), Hans Veerman, Guus Oster (Ben), Jan Retel (Cees), Hidde Maas (Arie), Leontien Ceulemans (Tine), Riek Schagen, Maarten Spanjer.

Spetters *(1980)*
Crew: *Director* Paul Verhoeven, *Writer* Gerard Soeteman, *Producer* Joop van den Ende, *Music* Ton Scherpenzeel & Kayak, *Cinematographer* Jost Vacano, *Editor* Ine Schenkkan, *Production Designer* Dick Schillemans, Colour, 115 minutes.
Cast: Hans van Tongeren (Rien), Renée Soutendijk (Fientje), Toon Agterberg (Eef), Maarten Spanjer (Hans), Marianne Boyer (Maya), Peter Tuinman (Jaap, Fientje's Brother), Saskia Ten Batenburg (Truus), Yvonne Valkenburg (Annette), Ab Abspoel (Father of Rien), Rudi Falkenhagen (Wout, Hans' Father), Hans Veerman (Willem, Eef's Father), Ben Aerden (Old Homosexual), Kitty Courbois (Doctor), Gees Linnebank (Homosexual), Hugo Metsers (Hell's Angel), Peter Oosthoek (Priest), Jeroen Krabbé (Frans Henkhof), Rutger Hauer (Gerrit Witkamp).

FLESH+BLOOD

(Episode 21 of The Hitchhiker, 1986)
Crew: *Director* Paul Verhoeven, Colour, 26 minutes.
Cast: Nicholas Campbell (The Hitchhiker), Peter Coyote (Alex), LeGena Hart (Leda Bidel)

RoboCop *(1987)*

Crew: *Director* Paul Verhoeven, *Writers* Edward Neumeier & Michael Miner, *Executive Producer* Jon Davison, *Producer* Arne Schmidt, *Music* Basil Poledouris, *Cinematographer* Jost Vacano, *Editor* Frank J. Urioste, *Production Designer* William Sandell, *RoboCop Creator* Rob Bottin, *ED-209 Sequences Creator* Phil Tippett, Colour, 103 minutes.
Cast: Peter Weller (Officer Alex J. Murphy/RoboCop), Nancy Allen (Officer Anne Lewis), Daniel O'Herlily (The Old Man), Ronny Cox (Dick Jones), Kurtwood Smith (Clarence Boddicker), Miguel Ferrer (Bob Morton), Robert DoQui (Sergeant Warren Reed), Ray Wise (Leon Nash), Felton Perry (Johnson), Paul McCrane (Emil Antonowsky), Del Zamora (Kaplan), Leeza Gibbons (Jesse Perkins), Jon Davison (Voice of ED-209).

Total Recall *(1990)*

Crew: *Director* Paul Verhoeven, *Writers* Ronald Shusett, Dan O'Bannon & Gary Goldman, *Short Story* "We Can Remember It for You Wholesale" Philip K. Dick, *Executive Producers* Mario Kassar & Andrew Vajna, *Producers* Buzz Feitshans and Ronald Shusett, *Music* Jerry Goldsmith, *Cinematographer* Jost Vacano, *Editor* Frank J. Urioste, *Production Designer* William Sandell, *Special Make-Up Effects Designer* Rob Bottin, *Visual Effects Supervisor* Eric Brevig Colour, 109 minutes.

The Fourth Man *(De Vierde Man, 1983)*

Crew: *Director* Paul Verhoeven, *Writer* Gerard Soeteman, *Novel* Gerard Reve, *Producer* Rob Houwer, *Music* Loek Dikker, *Cinematographer* Jan de Bont, *Editor* Ine Schenkkan, *Art Director* Roland de Groot, Colour, 90 minutes.
Cast: Jeroen Krabbé (Gerard Reve), Renée Soutendijk (Christine Halslag), Thom Hoffman (Herman), Dolf de Vries (Dr. de Vries), Geert de Jong (Ria), Hans Veerman (Undertaker), Hero Muller (Josefs), Caroline de Beus (Adrienne), Reinout Bussemaker (First Husband), Erik J. Meijer (Second Husband), Ursul de Geer (Third Husband), Filip Bolluyt (Surfer).

Flesh+Blood

(The Rose and the Sword, 1985)
Crew: *Director* Paul Verhoeven, *Writer* Gerard Soeteman & Paul Verhoeven, *Story* Gerard Soeteman, *Producer* Gijs Versluys, *Music* Basil Poledouris, *Cinematographer* Jan de Bont, *Editor* Ine Schenkkan, *Art Director* Felix Murcia, *Costumes* Yvonne Blake, Colour, 126 minutes.
Cast: Rutger Hauer (Martin), Jennifer Jason Leigh (Agnes), Tom Burlinson (Steven), Jack Thompson (Hawkwood), Fernando Hilbeck (Arnolfini), Susan Tyrrell (Celine), Ronald Lacey (Cardinal), Brion James (Karsthans), John Dennis Johnston (Summer), Simon Andreu (Miel), Bruno Kirby (Orbec), Kitty Courbois (Anna), Marina Saura (Polly), Hans Veerman (Father George), Jake Wood (Little John).

Cast: Arnold Schwarzenegger (Douglas Quaid), Rachel Ticotin (Melina), Sharon Stone (Lori), Ronny Cox (Vilos Cohaagen), Michael Ironside (Richter), Marshall Bell (George/Kuato), Mel Johnson Jr. (Benny), Michael Champion (Helm), Roy Brocksmith (Dr. Edgemar), Ray Baker (Bob McClane), Rosemary Dunsmore (Dr. Lull), David Knell (Ernie), Alexia Robinson (Tiffany), Dean Norris (Tony), Mark Carlton (Bartender), Debbie Lee Carrington (Thumbelina), Priscilla Allen (Fat Lady), Monica Steuer (Mutant Mother), Sasha Rionda (Mutant Child), Robert Picardo (Voice of Johnnycab).

Basic Instinct (1992)

Crew: *Director* Paul Verhoeven, *Writer* Joe Eszterhas, *Executive Producer* Mario Kassar, *Producer* Alan Marshall, *Music* Jerry Goldsmith, *Cinematographer* Jan de Bont, *Editor* Frank J. Urioste, *Production Designer* Terence Marsh, *Special Effects* Rob Bottin, Colour, 130 minutes.
Cast: Michael Douglas (Det. Nick Curran), Sharon Stone (Catherine Tramell), George Dzundza (Gus Moran), Jeanne Tripplehorn (Dr. Beth Garner), Denis Arndt (Lt. Philip Walker), Leilani Sarelle (Roxy), Bruce A. Young (Andrews), Chelcie Ross (Capt. Talcott), Dorothy Malone (Hazel Dobkins), Wayne Knight (John Correli), Daniel von Bargen (Lt. Marty Nilsen), Stephen Tobolowsky (Dr. Lamott), Benjamin Mouton (Harrigan), Jack McGee (Sheriff), Bill Cable (Johnny Boz).

Showgirls (1995)

Crew: *Director* Paul Verhoeven, *Writer* Joe Eszterhas, *Executive Producer* Mario Kassar, *Producer* Alan Marshall, *Co-Producers* Charles Evans and Ben Myron, *Music* David A. Stewart, *Cinematographer* Jost Vacano, *Editors* Mark Goldblatt & Mark Helfrich, *Production Designer*

Allan Cameron, *Costumes* Ellen Mirojnick, *Choreographer* Marguerite Pomerhn-Derricks, Colour, 131 minutes.
Cast: Elizabeth Berkley (Nomi Malone), Kyle MacLachlan (Zack Carcy), Gina Gershon (Cristal Connors), Glenn Plummer (James Smith), Robert Davi (Al Torres), Alan Rachins (Tony Moss), Gina Ravera (Molly Abrams), Lin Tucci (Henrietta "Mama" Bazoom), Greg Travis (Phil Newkirk), Al Ruscio (Mr. Karlman), Patrick Bristow (Marty Jacobsen), William Shockley (Andrew Carver).

Starship Troopers (1997)

Crew: *Director* Paul Verhoeven, *Writer* Ed Neumeier, *Novel* Robert Heinlein, *Producers* Alan Marshall & Jon Davison, *Co-Producer* Ed Neumeier, *Music* Basil Poledouris, *Cinematographer* Jost Vacano, *Editor* Mark Goldblatt, *Production Designer* Allan Cameron, *Costumes* Ellen Mirojnick, *Special Effects Supervisor* John Richardson, *Creature Visual Effects Supervisor* Phil Tippett, *Insect Designer* Craig Hayes, *Spaceship Visual Effects Supervisor* Scott E. Anderson, *Mr. Busey's Violin Coach* Martine Verhoeven, *Compositor* Helen Verhoeven.
Cast: Casper Van Dien (Johnny Rico), Dina Meyer (Dizzy Flores), Denise Richards (Carmen Ibanez), Jake Busey (Pvt. Ace Levy), Neil Patrick Harris (Col. Carl Jenkins), Clancy Brown (Career Sgt. Zim), Seth Gillian (Pvt. Sugar Watkins), Patrick Muldoon (Zander Barcalow), Michael Ironside (Lt. Jean Rasczak), Rue McClanahan (Biology Teacher), Marshall Bell (General Owen), Eric Bruskotter (Breckinridge), Matt Levin (Kitten Smith), Blake Lindsley (Katrina McIntire), Anthony Michael Ruivivar (Shujumi), Capt. Deladier (Brenda Strong), Dean Norris (Major), Christopher Curry (Bill Rico, Johnny's Dad), Lenore Kasdorf (Mrs. Rico, Johnny's Mom), Tami-Adrian George (Djana'D), Teo (Cpl. Bronski), Steven Ford (Lt. Willy), Ungela

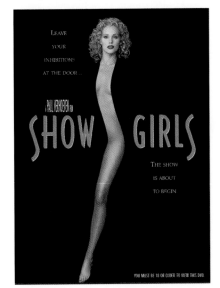

Brockman (Cpl. Birdie), Curnal Achilles Aulisio (Sgt. Gillespie), Greg Travis (Network Correspondent), Bruce Gray (Sky Marshal Dienes), Denise Dowse (Sky Marshal Tehat Meru), John Cunningham (Federation Network Announcer), Jon Davison (Buenos Aires Survivor), Edward Neumeier (Defendant), Zoe Poledouris (School Prom Lead Singer).

Hollow Man (2000)

Crew: *Director* Paul Verhoeven, *Writer* Andrew W. Marlowe, *Story* Gary Scott Thompson & Andrew W. Marlowe, *Executive Producer* Marion Rosenberg, *Producers* Alan Marshall & Douglas Wick, *Music* Jerry Goldsmith, *Cinematographer* Jost Vacano, *Editor* Mark Goldblatt, *Production Designer* Allan Cameron, *Special Effects Supervisor* Scott E. Anderson, *Visual Effects Supervisor* Craig Hayes, Colour, 112 minutes.
Cast: Elisabeth Shue (Linda McKay), Kevin Bacon (Sebastian Caine), Josh Brolin (Matthew Kensington), Kim Dickens (Sarah Kennedy), Greg Grunberg (Carter Abbey), Joey Slotnick (Frank Chase), Mary Randle (Janice Walton), William Devane (Dr. Howard Kramer), Rhona Mitra (Sebastian's Neighbour), Pablo Espinosa (Warehouse Guard), J. Patrick McCormack (Gen. Caster), Tom Woodruff Jr. (Isabelle the Gorilla), Gary Hecker (Gorilla Vocals)

Bibliography

Texts by Verhoeven
- 'Dizzying Blondes.' *Sight and Sound*, June 2002, pg. 62
- 'How to Shoot a Nude Scene.' *New York Times Magazine*, 3 November 2002, pg. 28
- *Showgirls: Portrait of a Film.* Newmarket 1995
- 'Time to Speak Out for Freedom of Expression.' *Times* (London), 14 March 1993

Interviews
- **Blokland, Robbert:** 'A Long Talk with Paul Verhoeven.' www.AintItCool.com, April 2002
- **Bouineau, Jean-Marc:** *Le Petit Livre de Paul Verhoeven.* SpartOrange 1994
- **Bouineau, Jean-Marc:** *Paul Verhoeven: Beyond Flesh and Blood.* Le Cinephage 2001
- **Bouzereau, Laurent:** *The Cutting Room Floor.* Citadel 1994
- **Cronenworth, Brian:** 'Man of Iron.' *American Film*, October 1987, pgs. 33-35
- **D'Amato, Brian & Rimanelli, David:** 'Dutchman's Breaches: Talk with Paul Verhoeven.' *Artforum*, Summer 2000, pgs. 150-55, 201
- **Florence, Bill:** 'Pumping Irony: *Total Recall*.' *Cinefantastique*, May 1990, pg. 54
- **Hickenlooper, George:** *Reel Conversations: Candid Interviews with Film's Foremost Directors and Critics.* Citadel 1991
- **Holben, Jay:** 'Invisible Force.' *American Cinematographer*, August 2000, pgs. 50-55
- **Koppl, Rudy:** 'Paul Verhoeven.' *Film Music*, February 1999, pgs. 38-40
- **Lim, Dennis:** 'Triumph of the Ill.' *Village Voice*, 22 August 2000, pgs. 61-63
- **McBride, Joseph:** 'Big Bugs! Big Bucks!' *The Director's Chair Interviews*, www.mrshowbiz.go.com 1997
- **Mendik, Xavier:** 'The (Un)Hollow Man: Paul Verhoeven Discusses the Politics of Pulp.' www.kamera.co.uk 2002
- **Puig, Claudia:** 'Paul Verhoeven Regroups.' *USA Today*, 7 November 1997, pg. 1D
- **Reid, Craig D.:** '*Hollow Man*: Paul Verhoeven, Parts I & II.' www.cinescape.com, August 2000
- **Roddick, Nick:** 'Verholloven Man.' www.urbancinefile.com.au, September 2000
- **Shea, Chris:** 'Paul Verhoeven: An Interview.' *Post Script*, Summer 1993, pgs. 3-24
- **Williams, Linda Ruth:** 'No Sex Please We're American.' *Sight and Sound*, January 2004, pgs. 18-20
- **Wilmington, Michael:** 'On Dangerous Ground.' *Film Comment*, July/August 1990, pgs. 24-29
- **Young, Neil:** 'The Many Dreams of Paul Verhoeven.' www.jigsawlounge.co.uk, 18 April 2002

Reviews, Articles, Analysis
- **Ascough, Richard S.:** 'Symbolic Power and Religious Impotence in Paul Verhoeven's *Spetters*.' *Journal of Religion and Film*, October 2003
- **Austin, Thomas:** "Desperate to See It': Straight Men Watching *Basic Instinct*.' *Identifying Hollywood's Audiences: Cultural Identity and the Movies.* Ed. Melvyn Stokes & Richard Maltby. BFI 1999
- **Battistini, Robert:** '*Basic Instinct*: Revisionist Hard-On, Hollywood Trash, or Feminist Hope?' *Cinefocus*, Spring 1992, pgs. 38-43
- **Cohan, Steven:** 'Censorship and Narrative Indeterminacy in *Basic Instinct*: 'You won't learn anything from me I don't want you to know.'' *Contemporary Hollywood Cinema*. Ed. Steve Neale & Murray Smith. Routledge 1998
- **Cohen, Michael:** 'Too Much Bacon: What's Visible in *Hollow Man*.' www.sensesofcinema.com, September 2000

- **Delap, Joe:** 'Media-Specific versus Interpretive Choices Affecting the Text-Transfer: Convergent Versions of *The Fourth Man*.' *Kodikas/Code*, January/June 1991, pgs. 75-82
- **Deleyto, Celestino:** 'The Margins of Pleasure: Female Monstrosity and Male Paranoia in *Basic Instinct*.' *Film Criticism*, Spring 1997, pgs. 20-42
- **Duvall, Daniel S.:** '*Total Recall*: A Long, Strange Trip.' *Creative Screenwriting*, November/December 1998, pgs. 31-34
- **Eby, Douglas:** '*Hollow Man*: Director Paul Verhoeven.' *Cinefantastique*, June 2000, pgs. 12-13
- **Eszterhas, Joe:** *American Rhapsody.* Knopf 2000
- **Freiberger, Erich D.:** 'In the Beginning Was the Act: *Basic Instinct* as the Cinematic Image of Freud's Death Drive.' *Literature and Psychology*, Winter 2000, pgs. 1-25
- **Glass, Fred:** 'The 'New Bad Future': *Robocop* and 1980s' Sci-Fi Films.' *Science as Culture* 5, Free Association Books 1989, pgs. 7-49
- **Glass Fred:** 'Totally Recalling Arnold: Sex and Violence in the New Bad Future.' *Film Quarterly*, Fall 1990, pgs. 2-13
- **Grady, Frank:** 'Arnoldian Humanism, or Amnesia and Autobiography in the Schwarzenegger Action Film.' *Cinema Journal*, Winter 2003, pgs. 41-56
- **Hart, Lynda:** *Fatal Women: Lesbian Sexuality and the Mark of Aggression.* Princeton University 1994
- **Hoberman, J.:** 'Fantastic Projections.' *Sight and Sound*, May 1992, pg. 4
- **Holmlund, Chris:** 'Cruisin' for a Bruisin': Hollywood's Deadly (Lesbian) Dolls.' *Cinema Journal*, Fall 1994, pgs. 31-51
- **Hunter, I. Q.:** 'Even Baser Instincts: Notes on *Hollow Man*.' *Intensities*, Spring 2003, www.cult-media.com
- **Hunter, I. Q.:** 'From SF to Sci-Fi: Paul Verhoeven's *Starship Troopers*.' *Writing and Cinema*. Ed. Jonathan Bignell. Longman 1999
- **Hunter, Stephen:** 'Goosestepping at the Movies: *Starship Troopers* and the Nazi Aesthetic.' *Washington Post*, 11 November 1997, pg. D1
- **Jeavons, Clyde:** Review of *Turkish Delight*. *Monthly Film Bulletin*, March 1974, pgs. 55-56
- **Jeffords, Susan:** *Hard Bodies: Hollywood Masculinity in the Reagan Era.* Rutgers University 1994
- **Keesey, Douglas:** 'They Kill for Love: Defining the Erotic Thriller as a Film Genre.' *CineAction*, Issue 56, 2001, pgs. 44-53
- **Lennick, Michael:** ""All Is Well": In Defense of *Starship Troopers*.' *Video Watchdog*, Issue 47, 1998, pgs. 44-49
- **Lyons, Charles:** 'We Are Not Invisible: Gays and Lesbians against *Basic Instinct*.' *The New Censors: Movies and the Culture Wars.* Temple University 1997
- **Martin, Ann (ed.):** '*Showgirls* Roundtable.' *Film Quarterly*, Spring 2003, pgs. 32-46
- **Miklitsch, Robert:** '*Total Recall*: Production, Revolution, Simulation-Alienation Effect.' *Camera Obscura*, September 1993/January 1994, pgs. 5-39
- **Mizejewski, Linda:** 'Total Recoil: The Schwarzenegger Body on Postmodern Mars.' *Post Script*, Summer 1993, pgs. 25-34
- **O'Hehir, Andrew:** 'Is the Director of *Total Recall* and *Hollow Man* a Pornographer, a Homophobe and a Misogynist – or a Misunderstood Genius Who's Been Defeated by His Own Contrary Nature?' www.salon.com, 1 August 2000
- **Prince, Stephen:** *Visions of Empire: Political Imagery in Contemporary American Film.* Praeger 1992
- **Rayns, Tony:** Review of *The Fourth Man*. *Monthly Film Bulletin*, August 1984, pgs. 252-53
- **Sammon, Paul M.:** 'I'd Buy That for a Hundred Dollars!: The Making of the Criterion Collection's *Robocop*.' *Video Watchdog*, Issue 29, 1995, pgs. 44-55

- **Sammon, Paul M.:** *The Making of Starship Troopers.* Boulevard Books 1997
- **Sammon, Paul M.:** 'Shooting *RoboCop*.' *Cinefex*, Issue 32, 1987
- **Sandler, Kevin S.:** 'The Naked Truth: *Showgirls* and the Fate of the X/NC-17 Rating.' *Cinema Journal*, Spring 2001, pgs. 69-93
- **Sova, Dawn B.:** *Forbidden Films: Censorship Histories of 125 Motion Pictures.* Checkmark Books 2001
- **Streible, Dan:** 'The Wonderful, Horrible Films of Paul Verhoeven.' *Bang Bang, Shoot Shoot!: Essays on Guns and Popular Culture.* 2nd ed. Ed. Murray Pomerance and John Sakeris. Pearson Education 2000
- **Tasker, Yvonne:** *Spectacular Bodies: Gender, Genre and the Action Cinema.* Routledge 1993
- **Van Scheers, Rob:** *Paul Verhoeven.* Trans. Aletta Stevens. Faber and Faber 1997
- **Wagner, Chuck:** '*Hollow Man*: Invisibility Effects.' *Cinefantastique*, October 2000, pgs. 56-58
- **Williams, Linda Ruth:** 'Nothing to Find.' *Sight and Sound*, January 1996, pgs. 28-30

Documentaries
- Anon.: The Making of RoboCop. 1987
- Anon.: The Making of Showgirls. 1995
- Anon.: The Making of Total Recall. 1990
- De Hert, Robbe & Thijssen, Willum. Op de fiets naar Hollywood. (Dutch) 1993
- Krom, Frank: Soldier of Orange Revisited. (Dutch) 2002
- Schwarz, Jeffrey: Blonde Poison: The Making of Basic Instinct. 2002
- Schwarz, Jeffrey: Death from Above: The Making of Starship Troopers. 2002
- Schwarz, Jeffrey: Fleshing Out the Hollow Man. 2000
- Schwarz, Jeffrey: Flesh+Steel: The Making of RoboCop. 2001
- Schwarz, Jeffrey: Imagining Total Recall. 2001

Websites
- www.paulverhoeven.net
- www.ghosts.org/verhoeven
- www.mrqe.com
- www.imdb.com

Acknowledgements

I would like to thank all my colleagues in the faculty, staff and administration at Cal Poly. Without the intellectually stimulating and emotionally supportive environment that they create, this project would not have been possible. I am especially grateful to John Harrington, who welcomed me to film teaching and shared his wisdom, resources and friendship. The members of the "lunch group" – Stacey Breitenbach, Jane Leaphart, and Mary Whiteford – have inspired me and kept me sane through the years. Connie Davis, Sue Otto, Kathy Severn and Katie Tool have been of invaluable assistance to me in more ways than I can ever enumerate. I could not have researched this book without the superb help provided by Linda Hauck, Michael Price and Janice Stone in the Interlibrary Loan Department of the Kennedy Library. Finally, I would like to thank Sheila Gold and JoEllen Victoreen, who were teachers in the truest sense; my parents Phyllis and Donald Keesey, who have always been there for me and ready to give whatever I needed; and my wife Helen Bailey, whose dedication knows no bounds and to whom this book is dedicated.

The editor would like to thank Ethel Seno and Nina Wiener for their help coordinating images in Los Angeles, Stacy Lumbrezer at Paul Verhoeven's office for her enthusiastic correspondence, and finally to Paul Verhoeven for his trust, cooperation and good humour.

Notes

1. **Lim, Dennis:** 'Triumph of the Ill.' *Village Voice*, 22 August 2000, pgs. 61-62.
2. **Rafferty, Terrence:** The Thing Happens: Ten Years of Writing about the Movies. Grove 1993, pg. 233.
3. **Thomson, David:** The New Biographical Dictionary of Film. Knopf 2002, pg. 895.
4. **Schickel, Richard:** 'Disappear!' *Time*, 7 August 2000, pg. 84.
5. **Monk, Claire:** *Sight and Sound*, January 1996, pg. 52.
6. **Corliss, Richard:** 'Valley of the Dulls.' *Time*, 2 October 1995, pg. 74.
7. **Holben, Jay:** 'Invisible Force.' *American Cinematographer*, August 2000, pg. 55.
8. **Verhoeven, Paul:** 'Time to Speak Out for Freedom of Expression.' *Times* (London), 14 March 1993.
9. **Van Scheers, Rob:** *Paul Verhoeven*. Trans. Aletta Stevens. Faber and Faber 1997, pg. 229.
10. **McBride, Joseph:** 'Big Bugs! Big Bucks!' *The Director's Chair Interviews*, www.mrshowbiz.go.com 1997.
11. **Bouzereau, Laurent:** *The Cutting Room Floor*. Citadel 1994, pg. 200.
12. **Bouineau, Jean-Marc:** *Paul Verhoeven: Beyond Flesh and Blood*. Le Cinephage 2001, pg. 70.
13. **Young, Neil:** 'The Many Dreams of Paul Verhoeven.' www.jigsawlounge.co.uk, 18 April 2002.
14. **Verhoeven, Paul:** *Showgirls: Portrait of a Film*. Newmarket 1995, pg. 14.
15. See note 11, pgs. 199-200.
16. See note 12, pg. 35.
17. See note 12, pg. 72.
18. **O'Hehir, Andrew:** 'Is the Director of *Total Recall* and *Hollow Man* a Pornographer, a Homophobe and a Misogynist – or a Misunderstood Genius Who's Been Defeated by His Own Contrary Nature?' www.salon.com, 1 August 2000.
19. See note 7.
20. Columbia/TriStar DVD of *Starship Troopers*.
21. See note 12, pg. 23.
22. See note 7.
23. **Sammon, Paul M.:** *The Making of Starship Troopers*. Boulevard Books 1997, pg. 65.
24. ibid., pgs. 123, 126.
25. See note 12, pg. 27.
26. See note 12, pg. 41.
27. **Shea, Chris:** 'Paul Verhoeven: An Interview.' *Post Script*, Summer 1993, pg. 20.
28. **Todd, Douglas:** Brave Souls: Writers and Artists Wrestle with God, Love, Death and the Things That Matter. Stoddart 1996, pg. 57.
29. See note 9, pg. 58.
30. See note 12, pg. 36.
31. See note 28, pg. 61.
32. **D'Amato, Brian & Rimanelli, David:** 'Dutchman's Breaches: Talk with Paul Verhoeven.' *Artforum*, Summer 2000, pg. 153.
33. See note 12, pg. 47.
34. **Macnab, Geoffrey:** Review of *Business Is Business*. *Sight and Sound*, August 2002, pg. 58.
35. See note 9, pg. 91.
36. Director's audiocommentary on the Anchor Bay DVD of *Turkish Delight*.
37. ibid.
38. Director's audiocommentary on the Anchor Bay DVD of *Katie Tippel*.
39. **Hickenlooper, George:** Reel Conversations: Candid Interviews with Film's Foremost Directors and Critics. Citadel 1991, pg. 261.
40. **Patterson, John:** 'Red-Hot Dutch.' *Guardian* (UK), 4 August 2000, pg. 2.
41. See note 9, pg. 176.
42. **Hartl, John:** '*Flesh and Blood* Is Stirring, Original Medieval Epic.' *Seattle Times*, 25 October 1985, pg. 26.
43. **Bouineau, Jean-Marc:** *Le Petit Livre de Paul Verhoeven*. SpartOrange 1994, pg. 99.

44. See note 9, pg. 177.
45. See note 40.
46. Columbia Pictures DVD of *Hollow Man*.
47. **Fischer, Paul:** 'If the Shue Fits.' www.darkhorizons.com 2000.
48. See note 20.
49. **Gorney, Cynthia:** 'The Man Behind *Robocop*.' *Washington Post* 10 August 1987, pg. D1.
50. See note 9, pg. 195.
51. **Mizejewski, Linda:** 'Action Bodies in Futurist Spaces: Bodybuilder Stardom as Special Effect.' *Alien Zone II: The Spaces of Science-Fiction Cinema*. Ed. Annette Kuhn. Verso 1999, pg. 156.
52. **Florence, Bill:** 'Pumping Irony: *Total Recall*.' *Cinefantastique*, May 1990, pg. 54.
53. **Corliss, Richard:** 'Mind Bending on Mars.' *Time*, 11 June 1990, pg. 85.
54. See note 9, pg. 219.
55. **Roddick, Nick:** 'Verholloven Man.' www.urbancinefile.com.au, September 2000.
56. See note 43, pg. 75.
57. See note 32, pg. 201.
58. ibid.
59. **Lyons, Charles:** 'We Are Not Invisible: Gays and Lesbians against *Basic Instinct*.' *The New Censors: Movies and the Culture Wars*. Temple University 1997, pg. 129.
60. **Holub, Kathy:** 'Ballistic Instinct.' *Premiere*, August 1991, pg. 84.
61. **Sova, Dawn B.:** *Forbidden Films: Censorship Histories of 125 Motion Pictures*. Checkmark Books 2001, pg. 36.
62. See note 11, pg. 215.
63. **Rickey, Carrie:** *Philadelphia Inquirer*, 20 March 1992.
64. **Ebert, Roger:** *Roger Ebert's Video Companion*. 1994 ed. Andrews and McMeel 1993, pg. 54.
65. **Hunter, Stephen:** Violent Screen. Bancroft Press 1995, pg. 47.
66. **Hoberman, J.:** 'Fantastic Projections.' *Sight and Sound*, May 1992, pg. 4.
67. **Taubin, Amy:** 'The Boys Who Cried Misogyny.' *Village Voice*, 28 April 1992, pg. 35.
68. **Picardie, Ruth:** 'Mad, Bad and Dangerous.' *New Statesman and Society*, 1 May 1992, pg. 36.
69. **Deleyto, Celestino:** 'The Margins of Pleasure: Female Monstrosity and Male Paranoia in *Basic Instinct*.' *Film Criticism*, Spring 1997, pg. 39.
70. See note 12, pg. 91.
71. See note 9, pg. 273.
72. **Sandler, Kevin S.:** 'The Naked Truth: *Showgirls* and the Fate of the X/NC-17 Rating.' *Cinema Journal*, Spring 2001, pg. 91 note 74.
73. ibid., pg. 81.
74. **Carroll, Jerry:** '*Showgirls* Goes All the Way.' *San Francisco Chronicle*, 17 September 1995, pg. 28.
75. **MacFarquhar, Larissa:** 'Start the Lava.' *Premiere*, October 1995, pg. 84.
76. ibid.
77. See note 5.
78. **Williams, Linda Ruth:** 'Nothing to Find.' *Sight and Sound*, January 1996, pg. 30.
79. **Schaefer, Eric:** '*Showgirls* Roundtable.' Ed. Ann Martin. *Film Quarterly*, Spring 2003, pg. 43.
80. **Lane, Anthony:** *Nobody's Perfect*. Knopf 2002, pg. 151.
81. **Lippit, Akira Mizuta:** '*Showgirls* Roundtable.' Ed. Ann Martin. *Film Quarterly*, Spring 2003, pg. 34.
82. **Tourtellotte, Bob:** 'Movie's Show-All Approach Stirs Controversy over Morality.' *Buffalo News*, 22 September 1995, pg. A3.
83. See note 9, pg. 272.
84. See note 6.
85. See note 9, pg. viii.
86. **Puig, Claudia:** 'Paul Verhoeven Regroups.' *USA Today*, 7 November 1997, pg. 1D.
87. See note 32, pg. 155.

88. See note 9, pg. 271.
89. See note 12, pg. 31.
90. See note 14, pg. 22.
91. **Duralde, Alonso:** 'Simply Irresistible.' *Advocate*, 30 September 2003, pg. 36.
92. **Waters, John:** '*Showgirls* Roundtable.' Ed. Ann Martin. *Film Quarterly*, Spring 2003, pg. 32.
93. **Williams, Linda:** '*Showgirls* Roundtable.' Ed. Ann Martin. *Film Quarterly*, Spring 2003, pg. 41.
94. **Shaw, Jessica:** 'Party Girls.' *Entertainment Weekly*, March 1996, pg. 21.
95. **Hunter, Stephen:** 'Goosestepping at the Movies: *Starship Troopers* and the Nazi Aesthetic.' *Washington Post*, 11 November 1997, pg. D1.
96. See note 1, pg. 62.
97. **Kehr, Dave:** '*Starship* Wages the War on Bugs Crawling with Violence.' *New York Daily News*, 7 November 1997, pg. 60.
98. See note 23, pg. 139.
99. **Kempley, Rita:** *Washington Post*, 7 November 1997, pg. D1.
100. **Rosenbaum, Jonathan:** 'Multinational Pest Control: Does American Cinema Still Exist?' *Film and Nationalism*. Ed. Alan Williams. Rutgers University 2002, pg. 226.
101. See note 23, pg. 149.
102. See note 12, pgs. 76, 79.
103. **Blokland, Robbert:** 'A Long Talk with Paul Verhoeven.' www.AintItCool.com, April 2002.
104. See note 13.
105. **Pinol, Christopher:** 'Paul Verhoeven – Interview.' Locarno International Film Festival. www.filmfestivals.com 2000.
106. See note 7, pg. 51.
107. **Reid, Craig D.:** '*Hollow Man*: Paul Verhoeven, Parts I & II.' www.cinescape.com, August 2000.
108. **Denby, David:** 'Nowhere to Go.' *New Yorker*, 14 August 2000, pg. 88.
109. 'A Talk with Paul Verhoeven.' www.dvdtalk.com 2000.
110. See note 7, pg. 51.
111. See note 1, pg. 62.
112. See note 110.
113. **Osborne, Bert:** 'Creative Loafing.' reeltime.cln.com, August 2000.
114. **Foyd, Nigel:** 'Invisible Ironies.' www.mymovies.net 2000.
115. See note 12, pg. 69.
116. **Morrow, Fiona:** 'If I Stay, There Will Be Trouble.' *Independent* (UK), 22 September 2000, pg. 12.
117. '*Robocop* Director Wants to Make a Film about Hitler.' www.ananova.com, 26 April 2001.
118. **Young, Neil:** 'Paul Verhoeven: Rebel for Hire.' *Independent* (UK), 14 June 2002.
119. See note 28, pg. 58.
120. See note 1, pg. 63.
121. **Nugent, Benjamin:** 'Vanity Fuhrer.' *Time*, 2 September 2002, pg. 83.
122. See note 12, pgs. 81-82.
123. **Doner, Jermeny:** 'The X Man.' www.papermag.com 2000.

PAGE 192

Paul Verhoeven and Arnold Schwarzenegger

Total Recall' was an enormous success, thanks to the teamwork of Paul and Arnold. Here they show their mutual thanks.